The Gadget Guru Says:

Don't Panic!

JUST FOLLOW THE STEP-BY-STEP DIRECTIONS IN THIS BOOK

HANGING THINGS:

Any heavy object can be hung from a plaster wall. Get yourself a toggle bolt—it works like a charm.

FIXING THINGS:

Turn on the switch and nothing happens? Electrical problems are easier to diagnose and repair than you think. Follow the steps in this book and you'll be shocked at the money you save.

MAINTAINING THINGS:

Did you know your hot water furnace has a filter? Replace it at least once a year to keep your system running well.

BUYING THINGS:

It's not the size of your tool box that counts, it's what's inside. Find out what tools you need and how to use 'em right.

The Gadget Guru's Make-It-Easy Guide to Home Repair

by Andy Pargh

WARNER BOOKS

A Time Warner Company

Warner Books, Inc.
1271 Avenue of the Americas,
New York, NY 10020

Visit our Website at http://pathfinder.com/twep

W A Time Warner Company

Printed in the United States of America
First Printing: July 1997

10 9 8 7 6 5 4 3 2 1

Library of Congress Cataloging-in-Publication Data

Pargh, Andy,
    The Gadget Guru's make-it-easy guide to home repair / Andy Pargh.
        p.   cm.
    Includes index.
    ISBN 0-446-67293-9
    1. Dwellings—Maintenance and repair—Amateurs' manuals.
    I. Title.
    TH4817.3.P374   1997
    643'.7—dc21
                                                            97-13223
                                                                CIP

Cover design by Diane Luger
Cover photo by Slick Lawson

Book design by Proteus Design
Illustrations by Refugio Romo, Aleks Rozens and Aldo Coppeli

To my Mom and Dad who taught me, "The harder you work, the luckier you get." And to John Lentz, my attorney, agent and friend who has proven to me that to be successful, you only have to work a half a day—and I can choose which twelve hours.

Putting together this book has been a group effort. I would like to thank my co-author, John P. Holms, whose background in home contracting and construction as well as his patience has been an invaluable asset.

To Jamie Raab and John Aherne of Warner Books, who not only gave me this opportunity, but have been the ones who kept this project moving forward, even in the face of adversity. Anyone who ever attempts the tiring process of publishing a book should be as lucky as I am to have these two folks running interference on the front lines.

Special thanks to the folks at Stanley Tools, Black and Decker, Skil, Moen, Owens-Corning, First Alert, Rubber-Maid and Lasko for their advice and support during the course of this project. And thanks as well for allowing us the use of their photographs, illustrations and other materials. Their generosity helped make this book possible.

And finally to my staff, the folks behind the scenes, who make sure that our syndicated newspaper column, *NBC Today* segments, magazine articles, Internet services, America On-Line forum and never-ending lists of new projects keep going and going and going.

If you have a question, comment or opinion about this book, send me a note via my Internet site at: http://www.gadgetguru.com

TABLE OF CONTENTS

Introduction

I've known Andy Pargh for the last five years. I first met him as the Gadget Guru on *Weekend Today*. When you meet Andy initially, you realize one thing immediately: he's a geek. Oh sure, he's got a Harley-Davidson, he has the latest boy's toys: stereos, computers, smart house . . . But, he's a geek. A very nice geek. A very knowledgeable geek. A well-informed geek. But the bottom line is . . . he's a geek.

How do I know this? Because I'm a geek too. I love techno-stuff. I love gadgets. When I was starting my website on the Internet, www.roker.com (shameless plug, but Andy ain't paying me for this, so I gotta get something outta the deal), I turned to Andy for information on hardware and software.

I enjoy finding weird little items that may not make life easier, but make it more interesting. Most of the stuff Andy brings to the viewers of the *Today* show are things that you don't need, but odds are, you want!!

What's the biblical saying? . . . And the geeks shall inherit the earth! So if you do not want to be left behind, you need to be a geek. Maybe not outwardly, but inside, you need to know the ways of the geek—whether it's in the world of computers, or as in this book, the ways of home repair.

Now normally, on the *Today* show, we don't let the Gadget Guru use sharp implements like power saws or screwdrivers. He could hurt himself or others, and our insurance rates are already painfully high.

But, Andy knows what widget or wang doodle is the best to help you repair that leaky faucet or fix that creaky door. The Gadget Guru, or Gadge Goo, as I like to call him, is the best at telling you how to get the most out of home repair. Although I give him a hard time, most of the time, the Gadge is the guy I always turn to when I have questions about what is the best power tool or tape measure or whatever I need, because the Gadge has this vast database of experts and manufacturers to tap into.

So if you're not a geek (or at least won't admit to being a geek) and you don't have access to a geek, and you need to know how to fix things around your domicile, then you need to read this book cover to cover. If you are a geek, you still need to read this book, because the Gadget Guru is the best. You will learn from the best. He is . . . KING OF THE GEEKS!! I bow in his presence, and you should too. Granted, it's a difficult position to read from, but it's worth it.

—Al Roker

PART ONE
Meeting Your House

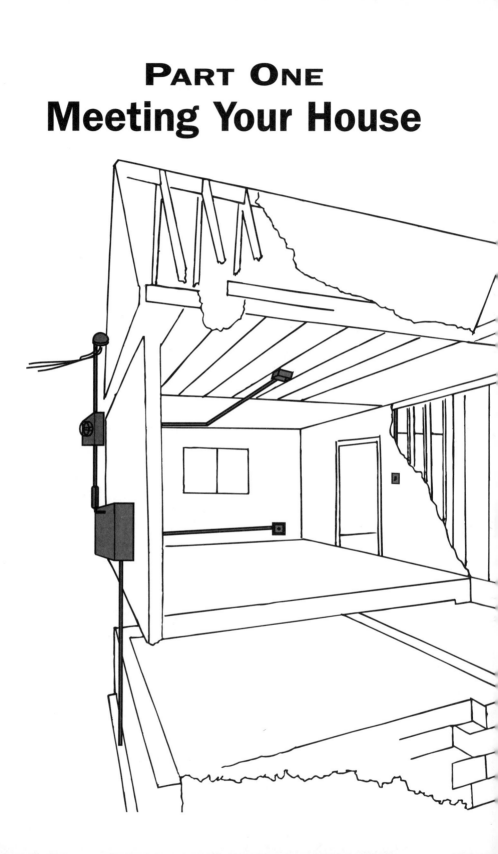

A Look at the Basic Systems And How They Work

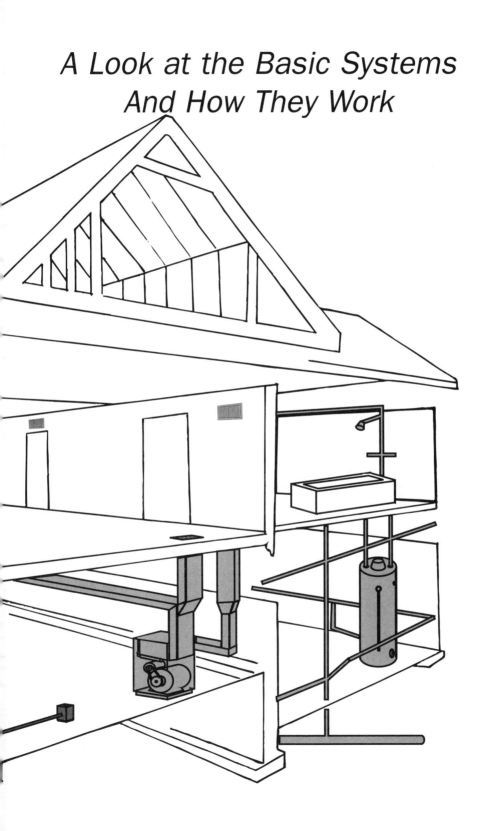

The first home improvement contractor was probably a Cro-Magnon who told his friends that for a decent price he could roll a stone up to the entrance of their cave to keep the animals out. The first architect was probably another friend who took a couple of skins for advising them that it should be granite instead of limestone. The first banker was probably another friend who said he could loan them the extra beads to get the job done but would need a little something for his trouble.

The first smart cave owners were people just like you and me who thought, wait a second, we can do this faster and cheaper ourselves.

We've come a long way from living in caves but a home still serves exactly the same purpose as it has for thousands and thousands of years. It provides safety, shelter and comfort for you and your family.

Make-It-Easy Tip #1

PUT TOGETHER A GENERAL HOUSE FILE

As you begin to meet your house I recommend taking notes and drawing maps that will remind you where things are and what they do so you can find them quickly and easily when you need to. A file is also a good place to keep the operation manuals, warranties, product updates, receipts and anything else that's vital to the operation of your home. It's also a good place to keep emergency phone numbers and the business cards of good craftsmen. Include a notebook that keeps a record of maintenance that needs to be done on a regular schedule as well.

And, in order for it to do its job properly, it's got to be taken care of.

The modern home is a combination of integrated systems that have to work together in perfect harmony to get the job done. As a whole it seems complicated, maybe even a little intimidating. **BUT ALWAYS REMEMBER, YOU DON'T HAVE TO KNOW HOW TO BUILD A HOUSE OR INSTALL A FURNACE TO TAKE GOOD CARE OF IT.** The truth is, once you understand how the individual systems work, you can also begin to see how things can go wrong, and what you can do about it when they do.

Let's take a look at the basic systems in your home and see what they're about.

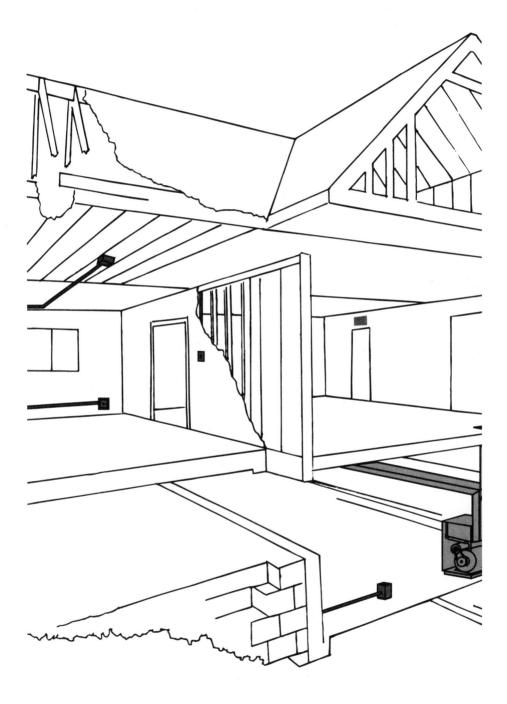

CHAPTER ONE

Give Me Shelter—
The Exterior and Interior
Revealed

All the exterior elements that make up a home—walls, siding, windows, doors and roofing—work together to provide a barrier between you and the elements. Your house is built to take all but the most extreme varieties of abuse that Mother Nature can deliver. Of course, there is no sure protection against hurricanes, flash floods, fires and earthquakes. But new technologies, products and building techniques have begun to make houses more stable and secure even in the face of these natural disasters. One of the fascinating things about the home building industry is how it adopts those new ideas as quickly as they come on the market and incorporates them into new homes.

Experience and common sense tell builders what works best in their area, and local building codes reflect the conditions that various regions offer. What works in earthquake prone San Francisco might not be appropriate in snowy Aspen. The majority of houses in Minnesota or Nebraska might have a basement, but they're rare in a lot of parts of Florida where if you dig too deep you'll drown.

Even with all the regional differences, houses in the United States have a great deal in common. Whatever their final exterior covering (wood, brick, stone, stucco or the various synthetic sidings) most homes have a skeleton frame of wood. The frame is covered with plywood or particleboard and foam insulating panels that are attached securely to a foundation, and is topped by a wood framed roof with some kind of shingling.

THE EXTERIOR REVEALED

THE FOUNDATION

If the house has a basement, the foundation will be a poured concrete or cement block perimeter wall. Often, if the house doesn't have a basement, a perimeter foundation will often rise just enough off the ground to create a crawl space. A foundation can also be a simple poured concrete slab. In any case, a piece of lumber called a **SILL,** specially treated to resist rot, is anchored to the foundation around the perimeter.

Your Basic Foundation

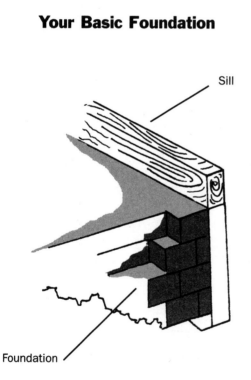

Sill

Foundation

THE FIRST FLOOR

Heavy wooden beams called **JOISTS** are laid across the span and secured to the sills. They are covered with sheets of plywood or some other panel product to form what is called a **SUB-FLOOR**. The subfloor will serve as a platform during construction and be covered with the finish flooring later.

When the subfloor is in place, the exterior walls are built and raised to form the first level. Wood is still the most popular material for framing exterior walls but the increasing cost of lumber is making builders consider other alternatives such as steel.

The frame accommodates all the necessary openings for windows and doors and is built to standardized specifications. Standardization takes advantage of the dimensions of existing building materials to cut costs and minimize waste. Standardized framing also allows all the other craftsmen like plumbers and electricians to know what to expect in the walls as they make their runs of pipe and cable. Everybody is working from the same page—and this will end up making basic repairs easier for you.

ADDING THE UPPER FLOORS

Once the first floor walls have been raised and secured in place, another series of joists are placed across the span and covered with a subfloor to create the base for the second floor of the house. The size of the lumber and materials specified for use are based on the load and stress they

---

Doing It Right—SAFETY, COST EFFECTIVENESS AND PROPER CONSTRUCTION TECHNIQUES GO HAND-IN-HAND

Tragedies can occur when builders or homeowners cut corners on construction or renovation to save a few dollars. Before you remove a wall you have to know whether it's helping to hold up the house. Before you add a fireplace or a wood stove you have to make sure that the floor will support the added weight. If you aren't sure, bring in an expert to advise you.

Do it right or don't do it at all is my motto—the price of thinking you can get away with less than what's required to save a few bucks is high. In other words, don't be penny wise and pound foolish—it'll cost you more in the long run. Local building codes define proper and legal construction practice very clearly. This is why you must follow building codes when you do major renovations and have a building permit to prove it.

must carry to keep the upper floors standing. You'll find that heavy-duty construction materials, such as beefy timbers and steel reinforcing, are used at the bottom and that lighter materials will be used as the structure rises. This is done to conserve weight without sacrificing strength and resiliency. It is also cost effective.

The process of raising walls and capping them with joists and subflooring is repeated until the house reaches its final level. Then the carpenters are ready to start framing out the roof. At this point another team is probably at work enclosing the bottom levels with whatever has been chosen for siding and adding exterior insulation if required.

THE ROOF

Architecturally, the roof is one of the most significant and visible design elements of a house. It's also the part of the house most exposed to the weather and it obviously takes the worst beating from rain, snow, wind and sun.

Modern roofs have several things in common regardless of their complexity or what's used to cover them. They're made of wooden framing

The GADGET Guru Make-It-Easy Tip #2

FIND OUT WHAT'S BEHIND THOSE WALLS

Before you begin any project that involves cutting a big hole in a wall, find out what's back there. The interior walls are full of things that run your home. You can tell a wall that may contain plumbing pipes because it might be thicker. Walls behind fixtures like sinks or washing machines are very likely to be hiding plumbing and electrical systems. If an air conditioning or heating vent is mounted on a wall you can be pretty certain there's a duct behind it. This is why contractors punch small holes before they hack away. The pros don't like surprises.

THE LAW OF GRAVITY

Water is your home's worst enemy. The long-term effects of even the smallest undiscovered leak will eventually cost you a bundle. Therefore all of the materials that comprise the outside of a house are put together to make use of the fact that water runs downhill. From the top of your roof to the foundation every element overlaps the one beneath it, allowing water to run away from the structure. When your house leaks you can be sure that running water has defeated one or more of the overlapping systems. Look for water damage around window sills and door frames, rotting shingles, and stains and dampness where the foundations meets the body of the house.

covered with exterior grade roofing panels called sheathing, followed by layers of waterproof roofing felt and the final covering, which may be made of asphalt, tile, grooved shake shingles, etc., depending upon the design of the house. The roof also incorporates a system of runoffs, gutters and drainspouts to move water quickly to the ground.

THE INTERIOR REVEALED

The interior walls and ceilings of your home not only divide the space inside into rooms, but also hide a lot of the internal mechanics such as plumbing and electrical runs, telephone, cable and security system wires. In addition, you'll find insulation, heating and cooling ducts and almost everything else you need to run the house, but don't want to see.

Wooden framing is still the most widely used method of construction but lightweight steel is quickly gaining popularity. The thickness of interior walls will vary depending on what has to go inside them. Walls that contain major plumbing, heating/cooling or electrical runs or that are primary load bearers will be thicker than walls that are simply used to define living spaces.

As in exterior construction, the interior framing is built to standardized measurements. The **STUDS** (no, I don't mean Al Roker or me), or vertical members of the wall, will be most often set on 16 or 24 inch centers.

You'll appreciate the fact that someone framed your walls on standardized centers when you're looking for a stud to hang a picture or put up a shelf.

Make-It-Easy Tip #3

THE EASY WAY TO FIND A STUD

In the old days, carpenters had to trust their judgment and their tape measure when they were trying to find a stud in a covered wall. It was often a matter of skill and a bit of luck along with a few extra holes in the wall. But no longer. There are several brands of electronic and magnetic stud finders on the market that make it easy to locate a stud. Basically they're little metal detectors that find the screws or nails in wooden studs or the metal studs themselves if that's what's been installed. Great gadgets.

A Peek inside Your Wall

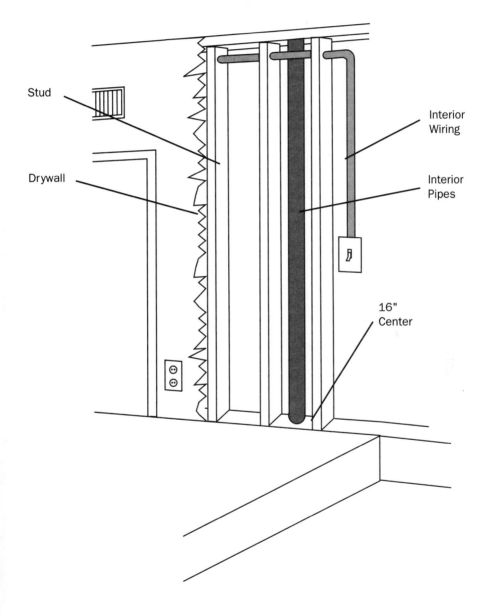

Stud

Drywall

Interior Wiring

Interior Pipes

16" Center

Once the frames are in place they are covered. Ceiling coverings are usually applied directly to the bottom of the joists that make up the upper floor. In the old days interior walls and ceilings were finished by applying plaster over strips of wooden lath which had been nailed to the studs or joists.

Today most interior walls are covered with prefabricated panels called **DRYWALL,** or Sheetrock, which consist of a plaster-like compound called gypsum sandwiched between heavy sheets of paper. Drywall panels are applied directly to the studs with screws or nails. The joints are sealed with paper or fiberglass tape and a plaster-like substance called joint compound. When done properly the final effect is almost identical to a plaster wall but twice as easy to do and infinitely cheaper. It's also easier to repair as you'll see later in this book.

Seeing Is Believing
CHECK OUT YOUR SHELL

Seeing is not only believing but also one of the quickest ways to understand how things work. After you finish this chapter you should take a little tour and see exactly how what we've talked about applies specifically to your home. Start in the basement and take a look at the foundation; see how the house is joined to it. Look at the floor joists and the subflooring for the first floor. Note all the electrical, plumbing and duct work and how it is attached to the joists and walls. Note the holes where plumbing pipes and electrical wiring are channeled upstairs. Make your way through the house, taking a look at the interior walls, especially where you have plumbing and electrical fixtures. Get up into the attic; if it's unfinished you'll be able to examine the framing and basic construction that hold your house together.

Now let's move on to the mechanical systems that make your home work. We'll start with how water that you *want* inside your house gets there by taking a look at the plumbing system.

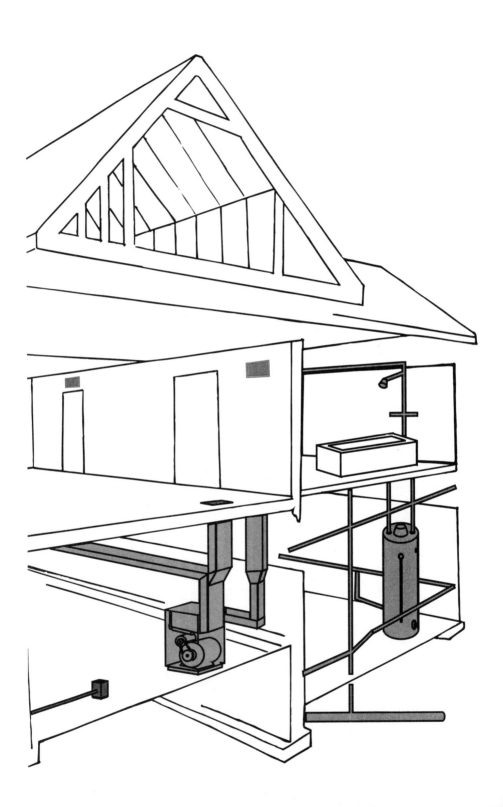

CHAPTER TWO

Things That Go
Drip in the Night—
The Plumbing System

Plumbing is all about the controlled and contained flow of water in and out of your home. Water comes in, goes where you need it to go and then it leaves—hopefully as quietly and easily as it came in.

A plumber friend once told me that all I needed to know about the art of plumbing was that *waste* (OK, he used a different word but this is a G-rated book) flowed downhill and payday's on Friday. He wasn't totally kidding; it's almost that simple.

IN THE PIPELINE—THREE INTEGRATED SYSTEMS

The plumbing in your home is divided into three basic systems.

The first is called the **SUPPLY** system, which brings fresh water, either from your well or municipal sources, into your home.

The supply system feeds water to a series of pipes in your house that bring water at the right pressure to service the second system, the **FIXTURES.**

The third system is called the **DRAINAGE** system, which uses the principle of gravity to carry the *waste* water from your home to the city sewer lines or the septic tank in your yard.

LEARN THE TERMINOLOGY

It's a good idea to spend a little time learning some of the basic terminology when you're going to get into repair, improvement and maintenance.

Why? It makes it easier to understand what the repair person or contractor is talking about. By using the right terms you may actually fool them into thinking you know what you're talking about—meaning they'll be less likely to take advantage. And, not having to call a washer "that little round rubber thing that goes in the faucet" saves time and embarrassment in the hardware store.

THE SUPPLY SYSTEM

Fresh water comes into your home either from your private well or the water company. Outside your house, the water company runs a branch off its main water pipe buried under the street with a shut-off valve, often buried in the ground, and a **WATER METER** to a connection inside your house. The meter tracks the amount of water flowing into your home in gallons and is the basis for your water bill. It's also the dividing line between what's owned by the utility and what you're responsible for. Sometimes the water meter will be inside your home, sometimes outside.

The connection on the *house* side of the meter, called your **MAIN SHUT-OFF VALVE**, is located somewhere in a corner of your basement. It's how you control the flow of water to every system in your home and it's where you shut the water off if a major emergency occurs.

Sometimes a second valve is found on the house side of the main shut-off valve. It's called a **GLOBAL** valve, and it's not only another shut-off for the main system, but also a means of controlling water pressure. The reason this is important is that the right water pressure is essential for your fixtures to function properly. Too little pressure, and they won't work at all. Too much, and at the very least you'll hear the water hammering through your pipes and at the worst they might burst. In which case your first stop is the main shut-off valve and the second is the telephone. Once the supply water is inside your home it's up to you and your plumber to get it where it needs to go. The first thing the plumbing contractor does is install a branch off the main feed (which is cold) to send a secondary main pipe to your water heater.

Then he runs parallel main feeds of hot and cold water that rise (why vertical plumbing lines are called *risers*) from the basement, through the walls toward the fixtures in your home like your sink or washing machine. If he's done his job right he's added a shut-off valve at every point a pipe branches off the main runs so that you can turn off the water on individual runs without having to shut down the whole system.

The supply feeds are primarily made of copper because it is resistant to corrosion, light in weight and easy to work with. Local codes in some areas, however, are allowing PB (Polybutylene) flexible plastic pipe for supply lines, because it can be cheaper than copper and is even easier to work with for most DIYs (Do-It-Yourselfers).

When fresh water, both hot and cold, has reached the fixtures and nothing leaks, the supply system has done its job.

THE FIXTURES

In plumbing jargon, **FIXTURES** are anything that require a feed of water, hot, cold or both, to work. Fixtures are sinks, bathtubs, toilets, dishwashers, washing machines, sprinkler systems and anything else that

THE PRESSURE'S ON

Water enters your home under pressure measured in *psi*, or POUNDS PER SQUARE INCH. The average entrance psi ranges from 35 to 100. Quite a variation. The happy medium is 40 to 50 psi. That's why a *global* valve that can step down high pressure to a more acceptable level could well be an advantage. If you don't have a gauge that tells you what the psi is you should consider having one installed so you can fine-tune the water pressure yourself.

connects permanently or temporarily to the supply and drainage systems. If you look under the sink, for instance, you will see a hot and cold water feed complete with individual shut-off valves. Every fixture in your home should have individual shut-offs so the water can be turned off for servicing, replacement or an emergency without having to shut down everything in the house.

The mechanical systems in the fixtures like faucets or what's inside your toilet tank all fall under the plumber's wrench as well.

Fixture supply lines are usually chromed copper tubing where they are visible, such as behind a freestanding sink, and plain copper in hidden locations, such as inside cabinetry.

THE DRAINAGE SYSTEM

The dirtiest job of controlling water in your home is done by the drains. A whole lot of things we'd rather forget about make their way down these hardworking pipes and some of them inevitably get stuck. Because it has the toughest job, the **DRAINAGE** system is the most tightly regulated by codes. Why? Because it controls the flow of waste out of your home and into the environment. It operates exclusively on gravity and depends on the unobstructed downhill flow of water to operate properly. It's also connected directly to the sewer line.

That's why each drain in your home contains what's called a **TRAP**. The trap is an "s" or "p" shaped tube that holds a barrier of water through which sewer gases can't pass, protecting us from noxious and possibly dangerous odors. If you've ever lost a ring in the drain, like I have, you know another very good reason for the trap.

Drains in each fixture connect to a large vertical pipe called a **STACK** that, in turn, connects to the main sewer line running below the house. Pipes also branch off the stack and run up through the roof *venting* sewer gases and balancing air pressure in the system so your toilet won't explode when you flush it. Large houses with several bathrooms may have more than one stack. It's essential that the vent openings on the roof don't become clogged with a bird's nest or other debris. Many local codes require a screen or cover of some kind to prevent such blockage from occurring.

CLEANOUT fittings will be found in several places on the main stack to make unclogging stopped up pipes easier, and a main cleanout will be found in the basement where the drainage system exits the house.

The pipes in the drainage system are usually the largest in diameter

Seeing Is Believing
CHECK OUT YOUR PLUMBING SYSTEM

Take a look around the house and identify the plumbing systems. Find out where the water meter and main shut-off valve live. Learn which direction turns the main on and which turns it off. An old plumber's trick is to paint or tape an arrow on the handle that points in the off direction so that you don't have to think about it in an emergency. It doesn't hurt to keep a flashlight handy as well.

Next check out the copper supply lines and see how they branch off the secondary mains and up to the fixtures. Find the shut-off valves both on the lines and near your fixtures. It doesn't hurt to make a map of where they are.

Trace the drainage runs, note where the cleanouts are. Go outside and find the places on your roof where the vents poke through.

Also note that if your home uses gas to run your furnace and other appliances the gas feeds are copper pipes and are another plumber's job.

and are still made mostly of cast iron because of its strength and durability. The problem with cast iron is that it's very difficult to work with. If codes allow, you will also find PVC (polyvinyl chloride) plastic pipe because it is strong too but much easier to work with.

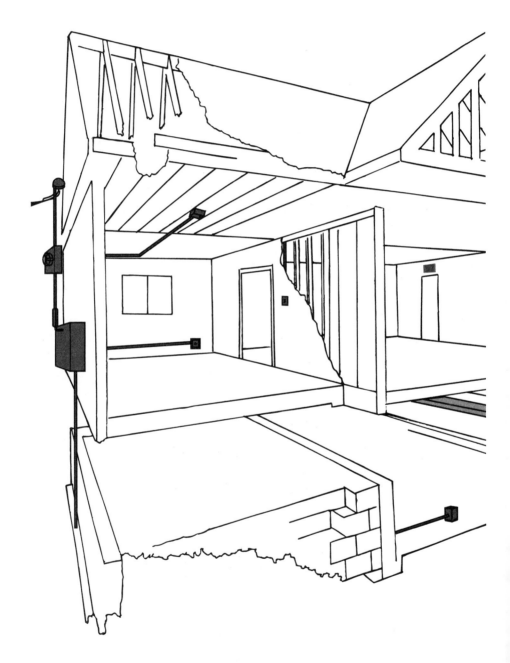

CHAPTER THREE

Making Sparks—
The Electrical System
in Action

If you've ever had the experience of searching for candles and matches in pitch darkness after a power failure you know exactly how vital your electrical system is. But most of us take electricity for granted, and when the lights go out, our first impulse is to call the electric company and complain. Of course when I've done that, I've usually just yelled at a recording but felt better anyway. Electricity is one of those things we expect to be there whenever we hit a light switch or plug in a vacuum cleaner. It's really a pretty simple proposition but the concept of how the electrical system works in our homes often seems difficult to grasp.

HARNESSING THE POWER—WHAT IS ELECTRICITY?

In truth, your electrical system is one of the most logical and simple systems to understand—and one of the most consistent. Electrical current always does exactly what it's supposed to do, and if you're careless it can hurt or even kill you. But if you know how it works, respect its power and follow some simple rules of safety and common sense, you can work with almost any of the electrical systems in your house with complete confidence.

IT'S A LOT LIKE PLUMBING

Your electrical system has a lot in common with your plumbing system. Wires and switches control and contain the flow of electrons just as pipes and faucets control and contain the flow of water. But the fact that they have things in common, however, doesn't mean they're the same. You wouldn't want to stand in a puddle and change a light bulb at the same time—unless you like to live on the edge.

RIVERS OF ELECTRONS

Electrons are particles of energy that are constantly in motion. Harnessing them is all about creating a closed system for them to move in. In the electrical world, that system is called a **CIRCUIT.** A circuit is simply a loop of wire called a **CONDUCTOR** that carries a flow of electrons called **CURRENT** from a generating source and back. That's why cables and extension cords have at least two wires in them—to create a circular path for the electrons to flow around.

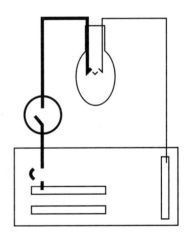

Electric current always takes the **PATH OF LEAST RESIS-TANCE**. Electrons will always flow through a larger wire (or object) before a smaller one. Some metals conduct electricity better than others. Copper wire has been proven to provide the least resistance and therefore is a better conductor than, say, iron or aluminum for creating circuits.

As long as the circuit is uninterrupted the electrons keep moving. But when the circuit is interrupted by any means at all, such as a switch, they stop until the circuit is completed again. When you turn a light switch on you complete the circuit, current flows into the fixture and the light goes on. When you break the circuit by flipping the switch, the light goes off.

If the circuit is broken by anything other than the switch (a frayed or broken wire, for instance) the current flows out of the loop and you have what is known as a **SHORT**, or uncompleted circuit. The light won't go on no matter how many times you flip the switch.

THE ELECTRICAL BIG THREE— VOLTS, AMPS AND WATTS

VOLTAGE is the pressure that moves the electrons around the circuit, like water is moved by a pump or by gravity.

AMPERES measure the flow of electrons through a circuit, just like the flow of water through your pipes is measured in gallons.

WATTS measure the power we draw from the electrical company to run our homes. A 100 watt bulb draws 100 watts from the circuit when it is operating at full capacity.

The longer the distance electrons have to travel along the conductor, the more voltage or pressure they need because a certain percentage of them are lost to **RESISTANCE** in the conductor. If you've ever run a really long extension cord to something and found it doesn't work to full capacity or the cord gets really hot, you've experienced resistance.

Researchers, engineers and the power companies developed standardized voltage levels to provide adequate service to our homes. That's why most electrical services operate at 120 volts (household needs) or 240 volts (major appliances).

Many applications such as doorbells and track lighting don't require as much voltage to operate efficiently, and manufacturers have developed **LOW VOLTAGE SYSTEMS** (usually 12 to 16 volts) to operate them. These systems require a transformer that *steps* the voltage down to the lower amount, saving power and, therefore, money.

THE ELECTRICAL SYSTEM REVEALED— WHAT WE TAKE FOR GRANTED

Electricity is generated at power stations by huge turbines. Then it's pumped, at very high voltage, to distribution stations. The distribution stations take the raw power, step it down with transformers to more manageable voltages, and send it on to a vast network of successively smaller systems that split it off to cities, rural areas and, ultimately, your home.

TALKING ABOUT FUSES AND BREAKERS

Circuit breakers and fuses are rated in amps. They're designed to "trip," or blow, if more current is demanded by the circuit than it is designed to supply. If you are consistently blowing fuses or tripping the breakers, it's a sign that you're overloading the system. Overloading can cause damage to appliances and fixtures and even start fires.

Circuit breakers have pretty much replaced Edison and time-delay-type screw-in fuses. Why? Circuit breakers don't have to be replaced. When they trip, they just have to be switched back on.

If your home is equipped with screw-in fuses and you'd like the convenience of circuit breakers, there's a way to get what you want without replacing the entire system. There are screw-in circuit breakers available to replace old style fuses. They cost a little more initially but they last longer and you don't have to go searching through every drawer in the house for that last spare fuse.

THE UTILITY POLE

If your electrical service is run aboveground, you can see the pole in the backyard. Sometimes it has a box, which is another transformer. Or sometimes the service wires just split off the main feed. Either way, you can see the wires running to the side of your house.

You can guess how much power you're getting by looking at the number of wires coming from the utility feed. If your home is older you probably see two—one black and one white—and your service is probably delivering 30 amps at 120 volts of pressure. Such 30/120 service has proven to be inadequate these days because of increased demand, and most modern homes are routinely provided with service of 60 to 200 amps at 120/240 volts. If you see two blacks and one white that's probably what you're getting.

If you don't see the electric pole, your service runs underground.

INTO YOUR HOME

The service connects to an electric meter which is provided
and owned by the utility company. The spinning dials record
the amount of watts (measured
in kilowatts) that flow into your
home and are the basis of your
electric bill. The meter is tagged
and sealed by the utility to prevent tampering.

From the meter, properly rated
service wires run into your
house and connect to the **MAIN
SERVICE PANEL.** The main
service panel, usually a gray
metal box somewhere in the
basement, is yet another distribution center.

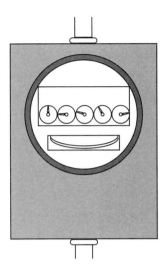

INSIDE THE BOX

In a newer home, the panel will contain the main disconnect as well as
a row of circuit breaker switches. They control the service that runs
throughout your home. In an older house it might contain only the

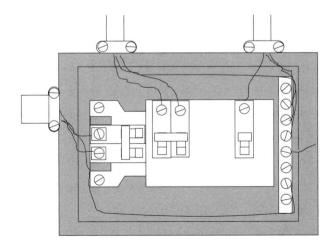

main disconnect, and the circuit breakers or fuses will appear in sub-panels at various locations around the house, such as closets, hallways or stairways.

With 60 amp 120/240 service you will see three wires coming into the panel. Two are black and are called the *hot* wires. They carry the electricity into your home. The white wire is called the *neutral* wire and completes the circuit, carrying the electricity away. You will also see a green wire (not part of the utility feed) which is called the *ground*. The green wire attaches to a grounding bus on the panel and runs into your house system along with the service and also to a copper rod buried in the ground outside or to metal plumbing pipes in the basement. The green wire is there to move any excess electricity away into the ground where it can't hurt anybody.

These colors are the same everywhere because they've been standardized by electrical codes so that there won't be any confusion over which wire is doing what job. Black is always *hot*, White is always *neutral* and green is always the *ground*.

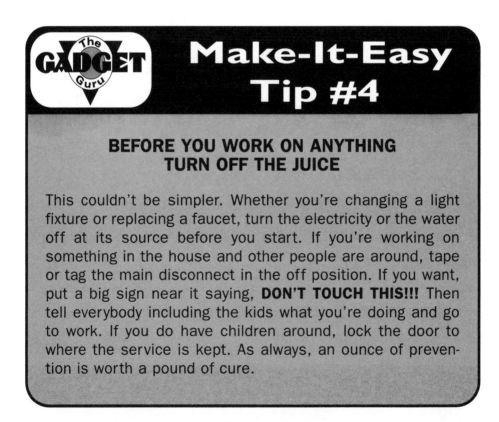

Make-It-Easy Tip #4

BEFORE YOU WORK ON ANYTHING TURN OFF THE JUICE

This couldn't be simpler. Whether you're changing a light fixture or replacing a faucet, turn the electricity or the water off at its source before you start. If you're working on something in the house and other people are around, tape or tag the main disconnect in the off position. If you want, put a big sign near it saying, **DON'T TOUCH THIS!!!** Then tell everybody including the kids what you're doing and go to work. If you do have children around, lock the door to where the service is kept. As always, an ounce of prevention is worth a pound of cure.

Safe Conduct
GROUNDING EXPLAINED

Electric current will always take the path of least resistance and if given a choice will always choose the largest object available. In the case of a bolt of lightning, the object can be a tree or a house. Sometimes in the home itself it can be a person—not the best choice from my point of view. **GROUNDING** protects us from becoming a conductor by providing the current an easier path through which to flow. The main ground wire that attaches to your main service panel is larger than the other wires so that it creates the path of least resistance if something goes wrong in the system.

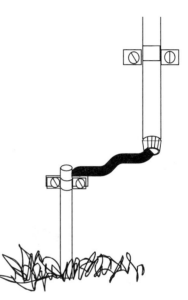

The main ground wire comes out of the panel and either attaches to a convenient plumbing pipe or runs outside to a copper *grounding rod* buried in the ground. Its job is to dissipate any *fault* current in the house safely into the ground. That's why it's called grounding. A lot of homes have both grounding systems. If you have lightning rods on the roof of your home, you know that they're there to create a safe path for the bolt of unharnessed current to travel if lightning strikes your house.

Having a proper and working grounding system in your home is essential to your safety.

LABEL YOUR CIRCUIT BREAKER PANEL

If your electrician hasn't done it already, you can save your-self a lot of time by labeling the circuit breakers in your main service panel. All you need is some tape you can write on, a black magic marker and a friend. Have your friend move through the house while you switch breakers on and off. Ask them to call out when a light or an appliance goes off upstairs and mark the breaker (living room, kitchen, refrigerator, etc.) appropriately. Also keep a circuit list in your general house file in case somebody pulls off the tape. (People can find the most amazing ways to be *helpful*.)

BRANCHING OUT

From the main service panel, wires branch out and run wherever they're needed throughout your house to supply current to switches, outlets, appliances and everything else that needs electricity to do its job. Depending on local codes, the wires may be run inside a type of metal tubing called **CONDUIT,** which is either flexible or rigid. In some places the wires can be run through walls without being enclosed in conduit.

Seeing Is Believing
CHECK OUT YOUR ELECTRICAL SYSTEM

Now's the time for another note taking tour to see how the electrical system moves through your house. Trace the feed from the utility pole to the side of your home. Take a good look at the electric meter and see where the feed comes inside. Examine the main service panel and see how the feeds come into it. Check out how they're attached to the main disconnect and then the breakers and how they are distributed from there into the rest of the house.

Most of the wiring upstairs will be buried in the walls so there won't be much to see except switches and outlets. But if a portion of your basement is unfinished that will be a good place to look for exposed electrical runs.

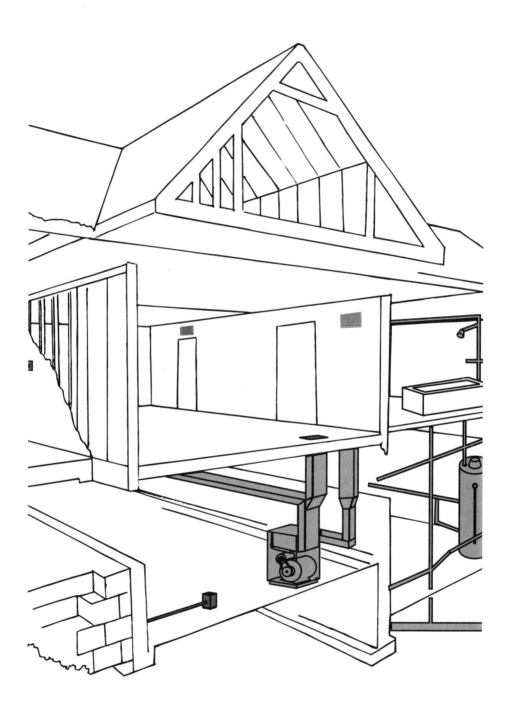

Chapter Four

Comfort Zones—
The Heating and Cooling
Systems Revealed

Whether you live in Miami or Minneapolis, electricity is electricity and plumbing is plumbing. There may be differences in how the systems are installed, maintained and cared for, but in both climates, the requirements are exactly the same. The lights need to go on when you flip the switch and the water has to flow when you turn on the faucet.

Heating and cooling systems, on the other hand, are specifically designed for the climate in which they have to operate. There's no other system in the home that has a more direct and constant effect on our quality of life. While we can tolerate extremes of heat and cold, we are most comfortable in a relatively narrow range of temperature—usually between 65 and 78 degrees with a moderate level of humidity.

That's the job of the comfort systems in the modern home, to keep the air temperature and humidity in an acceptable range. The heating and cooling systems must also be clean, safe, easy to maintain and energy efficient.

PROPER VENTILATION IS A MAJOR KEY

Your home must be well sealed and insulated and yet it must be properly ventilated to ensure a flow of fresh air. If a living space is too tightly sealed you are breathing air that is stale and potentially toxic. The volume of air should be changed several times a day without having to resort to opening doors and windows.

DEALING WITH HUMIDITY

Too much humidity not only makes you uncomfortable by decreasing your body's ability to release moisture, but has a damaging effect on your home as well. Paint blisters, wood rots, mold and mildew flourish in humid conditions. Too little humidity sucks the moisture out of everything and dries it out to the point that building materials shrink, causing cracks and splits. The dryness affects you as well, making for chafed skin, cracked lips and dry eyes.

New homes tend to be so tightly sealed that high humidity is a real problem. Older homes tend to be a little drafty and so dryness is a problem. Both issues can be addressed with a system that maintains the humidity at the proper levels and provides proper venting or insulating.

Weather in Your Home—
THE FACTS ABOUT
AIR, HEAT AND MOVEMENT

Air is always trying to seek a balance whether moving around in the upper atmosphere or moving around in your home. Warm air always moves toward colder air and vice versa. This is based on the old principle of gravity—cold air is heavier than warm air. The greater the difference in temperature, the faster the air moves, and that's what creates storms outside and drafts in the hallway.

In a closed system like your home, heated air rises to the ceiling and colder air will tend to gather at the floor unless there's a system in place to keep it circulating.

Heat moves in three ways:

RADIATION—A source such as the sun or a radiant heating device sends heat directly toward cooler objects such as houses or people. The objects absorb the heat and in turn radiate it toward other objects. Feel the sun warm your face on a chilly day—that's radiant heating in action.

CONDUCTION—Conduction is the movement of heat through solid objects. Interestingly, the denser and more solid the material, the faster the heat is conducted through it. Porous materials such as foamboard and fiberglass insulation slow the conduction of heat, keeping it inside longer.

CONVECTION—Convection accelerates the tendency of air to find a balance by creating a cycle of movement in which warm air rises and heats the space around it. As it cools it sinks to the surface to be warmed and then rises again. A forced air furnace works on the convection principle, and so do convection ovens.

DIFFERENT SYSTEMS—DIFFERENT NEEDS

Heating and cooling systems vary widely. They can be as simple as an electric baseboard heater or an air conditioner in the bedroom window. They can be as complex as a forced air distribution system, combining heating and cooling and a central humidifier. But no matter how sophisticated or simple, they have many things in common.

COMMON GROUND—THE HEATING SYSTEM

You'll find some variation of each of these elements in every heating system.

First, a **HEAT PRODUCER** such as a gas or oil burner or an electric heating element.

WHAT IS A THERMOSTAT???

A thermostat is basically a switch that turns itself on and off with a temperature sensor. The device is either mechanical or electronic.

In a mechanical thermostat, a metal coil expands when warm and contracts when cold. The movement trips a switch to turn on the heating or cooling unit.

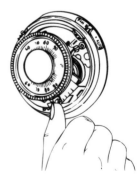

In an electronic thermostat there is programmable circuitry along with the coil that activates the switch and offers the user many options for timing the heat or cooling cycles. Essentially a small computer, an electronic thermostat can operate both systems with ease and savings in energy costs.

Second, a **HEAT EXCHANGER** such as a furnace where air is heated or a boiler where water is heated.

Third, a **HEAT DISTRIBUTION** system, usually a network of ducts and registers and returns that move heated air, or a network of pipes and radiators that circulate heated water.

Fourth, a **CONTROL** such as a thermostat to maintain the desired settings.

Common Ground—The Cooling System

You'll find some variation of each of these elements in every cooling system whether it's central air conditioning or a window mounted unit.

First, they are all powered by **ELECTRICITY**.

Second, they use a **REFRIGERANT,** such as freon, that circulates through a loop of copper coils to transfer heat from the inside of your home to the outside. The part of the **COIL** that runs outside is called the **CONDENSER;** the part that runs inside is called the **EVAPORATOR.**

Third, a **FAN** that blows across the coil, assists the heat exchange and distributes cool air through the house.

Fourth, a **DRAINAGE SYSTEM** to remove water that condenses during the exchange process.

Fifth, a **CONTROL** or thermostat to maintain the desired setting.

The Heating and Cooling Systems Combined

When central heating is combined with central air conditioning the systems most often share the furnace's air blower, duct network and filter. The thermostat controls both units.

HEATING AND COOLING SYSTEMS IN ACTION

Forced Air Distribution

Forced air systems work on the principle we mentioned earlier—cold air is heavy and sinks while warm air is lighter and therefore rises. Older furnaces relied simply on gravity to do their job. In modern furnaces the warm air is "forced" back into the house by a large fan. It works like this.

FUELING THE FIRE

The criteria for the many different fuels that can power heating systems are that they must be readily available, affordable, clean and energy efficient. The choice of energy differs from region to region based on these criteria. The most common fuels for heating are: fuel oil, natural gas, liquid propane gas, electricity, solid fuels such as wood and coal, and solar heat.

FUEL OIL—Oil burns cleanly and works well in any heating system. Prices can vary greatly depending on supply, however, and it must be delivered and stored in a tank.

NATURAL GAS—Natural gas is cleaner burning than oil, is more stable in price and doesn't have to be delivered or stored. The gas burner is also easier to maintain. It is more versatile than oil since it can also provide energy for ovens, stovetops, clothes dryers and other appliances.

LIQUID PROPANE GAS—Propane is used in rural areas. It provides the same benefits as natural gas except, like oil, it must be delivered to the site and stored in a tank.

ELECTRICITY—Although available everywhere and very clean it is most often too expensive to use as the primary energy source for a large heating system.

SOLID FUELS—Wood and coal were once the most common fuels used to power heating systems. While they are both still used, the emissions and residue from burning are high and there are strict environmental standards for their use.

SOLAR HEAT—In regions where it can be used effectively, solar heating is a popular, extremely economical and environmentally friendly means of heating a home.

Cold room air is pulled into a grate mounted in the first floor called a **COLD-AIR RETURN,** which feeds into the bottom of the furnace. From there it is heated in the furnace and filtered to remove dust and debris. The heated air is returned by the fan, or **BLOWER,** through sheetmetal **DUCTS** to **WARM-AIR REGISTERS** spread throughout the house. The cycle is governed by the **THERMOSTAT** and repeated as necessary to maintain the desired temperature.

A big advantage to a forced air system is that it can also accommodate a central air conditioning unit.

WATER DISTRIBUTION, OR RADIANT HYDRONIC HEATING

In a water distribution system, water is heated in a **BOILER** and distributed through a series of pipes to the radiating element. In older homes the boiler makes **STEAM** that runs to **RADIATORS** placed

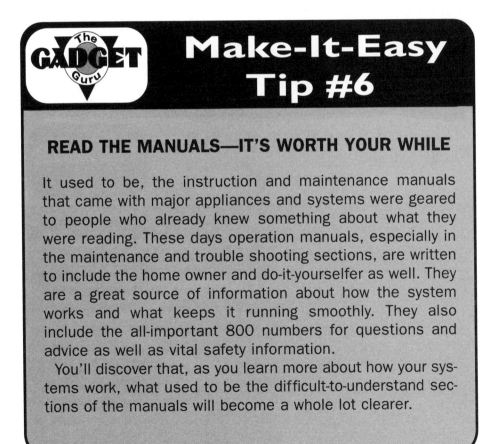

Make-It-Easy Tip #6

READ THE MANUALS—IT'S WORTH YOUR WHILE

It used to be, the instruction and maintenance manuals that came with major appliances and systems were geared to people who already knew something about what they were reading. These days operation manuals, especially in the maintenance and trouble shooting sections, are written to include the home owner and do-it-yourselfer as well. They are a great source of information about how the system works and what keeps it running smoothly. They also include the all-important 800 numbers for questions and advice as well as vital safety information.

You'll discover that, as you learn more about how your systems work, what used to be the difficult-to-understand sections of the manuals will become a whole lot clearer.

CHANGE THE FILTERS IN YOUR HEATING AND COOLING SYSTEM— *Pay Me Now, Pay Me Later*

When I moved into my new (new to me, but older) home I found an expensive surprise lurking in my heating system. It seemed that the former owners had never bothered to clean or change the filter in the furnace. Not only was it clogged with dust and debris, but all the ducts in the house were filthy. The bill from the furnace company who came out and cleaned it up made maintaining my furnace filter on a regular basis look like a very smart proposition. It's essential for proper operation and it's one of the easiest maintenance tasks around the house. The manual that comes with your system will tell you what needs to be done and how often for maximum efficiency. If the filter needs to be replaced on a regular basis you'll very likely save money by buying filters in bulk from a discount home supply center rather than one at time from the local hardware store.

I'll go into a lot more detail about changing furnace filters in Chapter 8.

throughout the house. As the steam cools and vaporizes (or becomes liquid again) it is returned to the boiler for reheating and recycling. Early boilers were powered by coal or even wood. The majority of boilers still in use today have been converted to oil or gas.

In a modern version of radiant water heating, a loop of corrosion-proof pipes is laid directly in the floor and heated water is circulated, warming the floor itself. The advantage is very even heat distribution and the fact that there is no constantly moving air to stir up dust and debris.

The downside is that a water distribution system is totally closed and can't accommodate the addition of an air conditioning unit.

ELECTRIC HEATING

Contractors love electric heating because it's cheap to buy and simple to

FORCED AIR SYSTEM

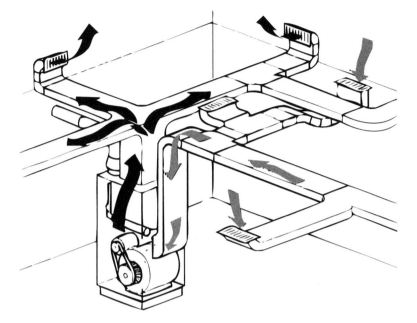

WATER DISTRIBUTION SYSTEM

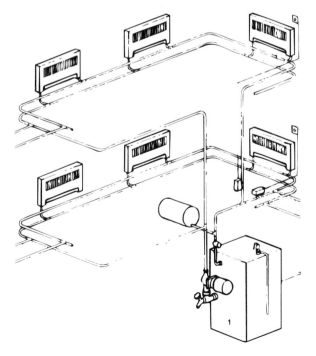

install. Consumers hate it because in most places it costs a fortune to run. While electric heat is useful in limited applications, such as small forced air units to help heat a bathroom, the high cost of operation makes it undesirable as a primary heating source in most of the country. However, in areas where the heating year is short and requirements are minimal, electric heat can be a good and inexpensive solution. And you can spend your money on air conditioning.

The units, mounted in the wall, along the baseboards or in laid coils or radiant foil in the floor, use the principle of **RESISTANCE** to produce heat. Electricity passes through an element designed to resist the flow of electrons, creating friction, and the resultant heat radiates off the element and into the room. Some electrical heaters have fans to help move the air.

FIREPLACES AND WOOD STOVES

For most of us fireplaces and wood stoves have become more of a luxury than a necessity—sitting in front of a roaring fire can be a pleasant way to spend a winter evening. For those who rely on them, however, huge gains in technology have made them more efficient heat producers.

Seeing Is Believing
CHECK OUT YOUR HEATING AND COOLING SYSTEMS

Take another tour of your home and see what your heating and cooling systems are comprised of, where they're located and how they move air through the house. Look over the furnace; if you don't know what kind of heating system you have, find out. Look at the air-conditioning system if you have one, and find out what it is and how it works. Trace the air ducts and see where they move up into the house. Upstairs find the registers and returns. Also note how electrical and/or plumbing runs are connected and in each case see how the disconnects work. Take notes and add them to your general house file.

PART TWO

Filling Your Tool Box— ## A Guide to Essential Tools

In toolspeak, the biggest difference between a rock and a hammer is that one has a handle to make the job easier, but both will still drive a stick into the ground. It's amazing to me that a lot of the basic hand tools (hammers, saws and knives) we use today are just fancy variations of those that have been around since people started to build things thousands of years ago. Over the centuries we've made refinements and improvements but carpenters from 12th century England would instantly recognize a modern handsaw or hammer and know exactly what to do with it. They'd also be amazed at how well made and easy they are to use, and my guess is that, just like me, they'd want to add them to their tool collection immediately.

The fact that the basic tools are still in use after all these years is a testament to two of my favorite concepts—*simple is good,* and *if it ain't broke, don't fix it.*

Now a trip to the tool section of any hardware store will tell you that there are hundreds of products on the shelves, and when you're filling your first tool box it can be a little intimidating. So I'm going to spend some time in the following section putting together a basic, bare bones list of tools you're going to need to do most of the repair and maintenance jobs around the house. Then I'll give you some tips on how to expand your collection as your skill and confidence levels grow.

You may not read and study everything in this section right away. But

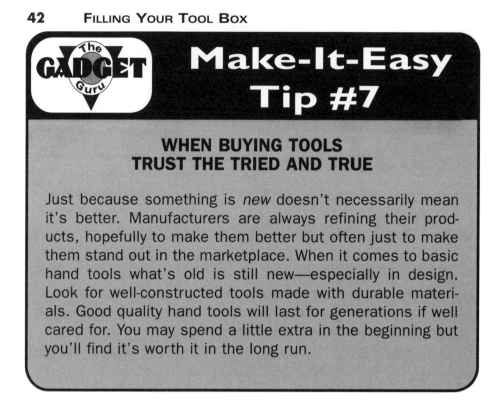

The Gadget Guru — Make-It-Easy Tip #7

WHEN BUYING TOOLS
TRUST THE TRIED AND TRUE

Just because something is *new* doesn't necessarily mean it's better. Manufacturers are always refining their products, hopefully to make them better but often just to make them stand out in the marketplace. When it comes to basic hand tools what's old is still new—especially in design. Look for well-constructed tools made with durable materials. Good quality hand tools will last for generations if well cared for. You may spend a little extra in the beginning but you'll find it's worth it in the long run.

I suggest you spend enough time with it to see what you need for a basic tool kit. Later when you start looking at home repair projects you'll find it an invaluable reference guide.

CHAPTER FIVE

A Basic Tool Box—
What You Need to Get
the Job Done

The oldest saw (pun intended) in the business is that you need "the right tool for the right job." The right tool used properly is almost always the difference between repairing something quickly and easily and spending a couple of annoying hours bruising knuckles, swearing at the dog and still not getting the job done. Many people I've talked to have told me the frustration of not being able to fix something can lead to the conclusion that the whole idea of home repair is impossible and better left to the professionals. Of course, nothing is further from the truth. Understanding the problem and then having a step-by-step plan of attack and the **RIGHT TOOLS** are the keys to making home repair and maintenance easy and satisfying.

On the following pages I'm going to identify and explain basic tools and put together a basic home repair and maintenance kit. Then I'll make some suggestions for expanding it. In the chapters that follow I'll identify special tools needed for individual projects.

The key here is that you don't have to rush to the store and buy everything at once. All you need are the tools to get you started on whatever project you want to do first.

I like the idea of building a tool kit on a project-by-project basis because it spreads out the initial cost and you wind up with tools you're actually going to use. As you look over the projects you'll notice that most hand tools are used over and over again, which winds up saving you money in the long run.

It's very likely that you already have some of these tools around the house. If so you'll simply be adding things to your existing tool collection.

STOCKING UP ON TOOLS— HOW MUCH TO SPEND?

This is always a difficult question. Like anything else, the better the quality of a tool, the more it costs. On the other hand, the better the quality, the better it works and the longer it lasts. The bins at the counters of hardware outlets are full of cheaply made tools of all descriptions, and sometimes in a pinch it doesn't matter how long that 29 cent screwdriver will last. But over the long haul you get what you pay for, and when you expect to use a tool for a long time, I think you should buy the best you can afford.

That doesn't mean that everything needs to be top of the line. Mid-range tools are usually more than adequate for home projects, and if you shop the discount houses and look for sales you can find real quality at reasonable prices. It does pay to shop around a bit because prices vary greatly from store to store. The biggest discounts will often be found through mail order outlets but you have to know exactly what you want and you have to wait for it to arrive. Some mail order houses do offer overnight shipping, but make sure the shipping cost doesn't make it more expensive than shopping at the corner store.

Of course, tools make great additions to wish lists so don't forget to let others know what you're missing. I remember when my cousin got engaged, his fiancée registered for china and silverware and he registered at Home Depot. My wife-to-be was far less understanding, which probably explains why I'm single today.

Make-It-Easy Tip #8

The GADGET Guru

BASIC BASICS—SELECTING A TOOL BOX

Tools are heavy, and lugging them around the house from project to project can get to be a real bore. You need a box that you can take from place to place without subsidizing your chiropractor. Not only that, but it's important to choose one that allows you to organize the tools and hardware so you can get to things easily. Remember that the box doesn't have to hold everything. Some tools will be just too big and would make the box too large to be practical. When you select a tool box keep a few things in mind.

1) The professionals often choose metal boxes because they tend to toss them around in the back of their pickups, and the durability and strength more than make up for the expense. You can save a lot of money, however, by investing in one of the modern tool boxes made of lightweight and durable plastic that will serve the home repair person very well. Some of them are on wheels, double as stepping stools and have built-in extension cords. Tools and tool boxes are very personal items so shop around until you find the one you love.

2) Look for a box with a removable tray. This allows you to carry just what you're going to need to do the job at hand.

3) Compartments like sliding drawers or ones that have individual lids are great for storing all the little things that can easily get lost in the bottom of the box. There's nothing more frustrating than pushing tools around to find a screw or a washer and stabbing yourself with a nail or razor blade.

FISHING TACKLE BOXES
HOLD HARDWARE WITH EASE

If you've got an old fishing tackle box around the house, you might use it to start holding your tools. Also clear compartmentalized plastic boxes with locking lids are perfect for storing screws, nails, washers and anything else that can get lost in a tool box. If you can't find what you want at the hardware outlet try a sporting goods or plastics store. The boxes are inexpensive and really help with organization.

But if you're really starting from scratch it might be worth a look at some all-in-one tool kits—tool boxes filled with the basics like hammers and screwdrivers. While they don't have everything you need, you'll probably find enough tools to get you started at a reasonable price.

It's a good idea to decide where the tool box and tools are going to be stored. A corner of the basement or garage is perfect. You'll always know where things are and you've got some space to hang tools that are too large for the box. The more organized you are, the easier it'll be to get things done.

A PLACE TO START—
BUILDING THE BASIC TOOL KIT

Most of us think that the only necessary tools are a hammer, a screwdriver, a pair of pliers and maybe a tape measure. If you went around your neighborhood and did a little survey of the tools in ten do-it-yourselfers' tool boxes, you'd find a lot of differences (tools are very personal things) but you'd also find a lot of similarities. And if you asked them to name the tools they used most of the time when they worked around the house, you'd probably come up with a list pretty close to this. If you're serious about saving time and money with home repair, here's what you're going to need.

The Gadget Guru's
Basic Tool Checklist

____Adjustable or Crescent
     Wrench

____Allen Wrenches

____Carpenter's Pencils

____Circuit Tester

____Claw Hammer

____Combination Saw

____Combination Square

____Continuity Tester

____Electric Screwdriver

____Electrician's Tape

____Extension Cord

____Flashlight

____Flat Pry Bar

____Florist's Wire

____Hacksaw

____Locking Tape Measure

____Masking Tape

____Mat or Utility Knife

____Pliers

____Plumber's Helper
     (Plunger)

____Putty Knife

____Screwdrivers

____Torpedo Level

____Utility Scissors

____Wire Strippers

The Gadget Guru's
List of Basic Hand Tools Defined

ADJUSTABLE or CRESCENT WRENCH Adjustable wrenches are multi-purpose tools for removing and tightening nuts. The jaw of the wrench is closed or opened by turning the threaded auger in the head. The 8 inch variety will do quite well for most household chores.

ALLEN WRENCHES You'll find that a goodly number of appliances are joined together with what are called *set* screws. And sometimes things are adjusted by turning set screws. A set screw is loosened or tightened by inserting an Allen wrench. Allen wrenches are hex-shaped and come in sets with a variety of sizes. I like the kind where all the wrenches are fixed together in some way such as on a ring or in a holder so you can't lose them.

CARPENTER'S PENCILS These are special pencils that have wide, flat, soft leads which are good for marking on many different surfaces. The pencil itself is flat so it won't roll away.

CIRCUIT TESTER A tool used by electricians to check whether or not current (electricity) is present in an electrical circuit. When the tip is inserted into an outlet and touches a "live" terminal or wire, the light in the other end of the tester goes on. An electrical safety must. Use a circuit tester when you need to know whether or not the juice is "on."

CLAW HAMMER Hammers come in all shapes and sizes. What you're looking for is a standard carpenter's hammer with a curved claw. The claw is used to pull nails and as a prying tool. Sixteen ounces is a standard weight. You might also consider a lighter one for smaller projects. The handle can be wood, metal or fiberglass. Whatever it is, make sure you can grip it securely and that the head is tightly fixed on the handle.

COMBINATION BLADE HAND-SAW This handsaw is called a combination saw because you can use it to cut with or against the grain of the wood without splintering or damaging it. For small jobs a combination saw will work as well as a power model and is a lot safer for beginners.

COMBINATION SQUARE A hand square with a handle that slides back and forth on a metal ruler. It is another essential tool in a fixer's kit because it serves a variety of functions: it can mark a 45 or 90 degree angle, can measure up to 10 inches, and has a little level in the handle.

CONTINUITY TESTER A continuity tester is made up of a battery, a small lamp, and two wires with alligator clips. Unlike a circuit tester, which tests for electricity in the system, the continuity tester is used to test whether or not there is a fault in the hardware itself (like a switch or a receptacle). Also a must for working on electrical projects because sometimes things break or wear out.

ELECTRIC SCREWDRIVER I love battery powered electric screwdrivers and think they're one of the most useful tools in the home tool kit. They make fast work of most simple assembly and hanging operations. Usually they come with tips that are reversible; one end is slotted and the other is Phillips so you're covered for almost anything. All you have to do is remember to keep it charged.

ELECTRICIAN'S TAPE A black, non-conducting plastic tape used to cover and insulate bare wire connections.

EXTENSION CORD A heavy-duty extension cord at least 25 feet long is an essential part of the home tool kit.

FLASHLIGHT Keep a flash-light in the tool box so you don't have to stop whatever you're doing to find one. A great extra is Black and Decker's Snakelight. It wraps around anything and its flexibility is a real blessing when you're under a sink and need light and both hands at the same time.

FLAT PRY BAR A flat pry bar is very useful for prying things like shipping crates apart, removing tough nails and giving you a little extra leverage when you're trying to shift heavy objects.

FLORIST'S WIRE A thin gauge, flexible wire that is green in color and comes on a wooden spool. It is very useful for making small repairs of all types.

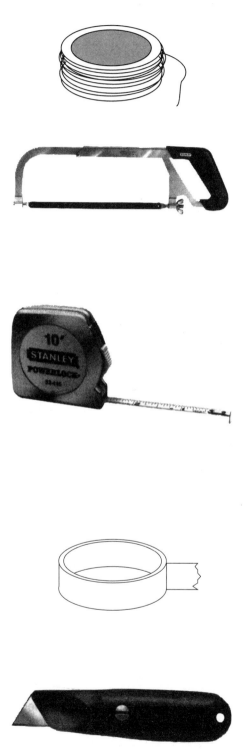

HACKSAW A saw used for cutting metal and plastic. Plumbers use them for fitting pipe, but they've got a lot of uses around the home. Special blades are made for different cutting jobs. The blades come in 8, 10 and 12 inch lengths.

LOCKING TAPE MEASURE Get a good quality 16 to 25 foot retractable metal tape measure with a ¾ inch blade. The stiffness of the blade helps you measure ceiling heights and the numbers are easily readable. The difference in price between one of good quality and a knock-off isn't enough to make buying the knock-off worth it. In the long run you'll be glad you bought the best.

MASKING TAPE A paper tape that comes in a large variety of widths. It's very useful for protecting surfaces while painting or repairing. It's also useful for keeping track of small screws and washers. Just lay out a length and press the small stuff into the adhesive.

MAT OR UTILITY KNIFE Sometimes called a razor knife. Mat knives have a retractable, razor-edged blade that will cut almost anything from carpet to electrical wire. The blades are replaceable and store in the handle of the knife. They are extremely sharp so be careful.

PLIERS Pliers are gripping or bending tools with two parts connected with a pivot to form both handles and jaws. Some are fixed jointed and some are slip jointed (to allow the jaws to open wider). You should have at least one fixed and one with slip jaws (the kind called channel locks or water pump pliers).

PLUMBER'S HAND SNAKE, OR AUGER There are three basic types of snakes which are used to break up clogs in drains. They all work on the same principle. You insert the snake into the drain and twist the crank. The wire turns in a corkscrew motion that breaks up the clog.

1) Coiled Drain Snake. The cheapest of the lot, it's a length of coiled wire that is attached to a simple handle.

2) Hand Snake. The coil is stored in a disk with a crank behind a pistol grip. The grip makes the snake easier to hold and therefore easier to use.

3) Closet Snake. This model is made especially for toilets. It's attached to a solid vinyl shaft so you don't scratch the toilet when you use it.

Snakes are very wise invest-

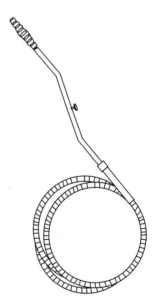

ments because plumbers charge a lot of money to unclog drains and it's a job you can almost always do yourself.

PLUMBER'S HELPER (PLUNGER) You've seen them, you may even already have one. Just make sure the diameter of the cup is larger than the diameter of the drain so you can get the suction necessary to move whatever's causing the clog.

PUTTY KNIFE Putty knives come in a wide variety of shapes and sizes and I like to think of them as the ultimate utility tool. They scrape, fill, pry and dig into lots of different places and they're inexpensive so they can be easily replaced.

SCREWDRIVERS A complete kit should include a variety of sizes, styles and lengths. Make sure you have a selection of **SLOTTED** and **PHILLIPS** heads. Most hardware stores sell kits that offer enough variety for most home repair projects. The advantage of Phillips head screws is that the tip won't slip off as easily.

TORPEDO LEVEL A small level, usually 6 to 9 inches in length. Levels are essentially straight edges with inset glass vials. The vials contain a bubble and are marked with two black

lines in the center. When the bubble falls between the two lines, whatever you've set it on is level (or true). It checks for level horizontally, vertically and at a 45 degree angle. A must for leveling shelves and making sure appliances are sitting correctly on the floor. Often one side is magnetized so you can hang it on the refrigerator and have both hands free to make adjustments.

UTILITY SCISSORS A medium quality pair of scissors will be useful for rough cutting of paper and other wrapping materials, including insulation. A pair in the tool box will also keep you from sneaking into the sewing drawer and using the good ones for things you shouldn't.

WIRE STRIPPERS A multipurpose electrical tool used to strip the insulation off wire so you can make connections. They also are used to measure the gauge or size of wire and serve as cutters.

THE GADGET GURU'S CHECKLIST OF BASIC EXTRAS

All the tools listed below are good additions to the basic kit on a project–by–project basis.

____Carpenter's Level

____Carpenter's Square, or Framing Square

____Carpenter's Awl

____Center Punch

____Chalk Line

____Clamps

____Cold Chisel

____Electric or Cordless Drill

____Hot Glue Gun

____Nail Set

____Penetrating Oil

____Pipe Wrenches

____Socket Wrench and Sockets

____Staple Gun

____Stud Finder

THE GADGET GURU'S LIST OF BASIC EXTRAS DEFINED

CARPENTER'S LEVEL A good carpenter's level should be at least two feet long and have replaceable vials.

CARPENTER'S SQUARE, OR FRAMING SQUARE A large metal square used to make sure everything's in 90 degree alignment.

CARPENTER'S AWL A carpenter's awl is like an ice pick with a rounded handle. It has many uses including marking the position for drilling holes, punching through drywall and scraping in confined spaces.

CENTER PUNCH A center punch marks a spot to be drilled with a small indentation. The indentation gives the drill bit a place to start and as a result the hole is exactly where you want it to be.

CHALK LINE A chalk line is used to make straight lines over long distances. String coated with chalk, usually blue, red or yellow, rolls out of a metal container. When the line is held taut and snapped it leaves a marking line. Very useful for making cut marks on plywood.

CLAMPS Having some clamps around is like having an extra hand whenever you need it. There are a lot of different kinds of clamps on the market, ranging from the very specialized to the very simple. In my opinion, the simplest, most versatile and least expensive are C-clamps with an adjustable screw on one end. You simply turn the screw until the material is held securely in place.

COLD CHISEL A cold chisel is used by plumbers to break up and remove old pipe and to cut metal rod. You also might find it useful if you ever have to break the nut off a bolt that is too rusted to remove any other way. It's also good for breaking up stone and cement blocks.

ELECTRIC OR CORDLESS DRILL   The modern electric drill is powerful, well balanced and easy to use. I personally love the cordless models for most home use; not having to drag a cord around is a real plus. A number of manufacturers have cordless systems with batteries that are interchangeable and power several different tools such as circular saws, hedge trimmers and the like. If you get a drill don't forget to get a combination of wood, steel and masonry bits. There are kits available that offer a starting mix of drill bits in handy containers.

HOT GLUE GUN Hot glue guns have so many uses around the home that you may come to wonder how you lived without one. Martha Stewart sure can't, she loves them so much that one Christmas she gave a gun to everyone on the *Today* show. Roker loved it but I'll bet ten-to-one that Katie and Bryant haven't taken theirs out of the box. There are many different kinds of adhesive sticks available. Just remember that it's called "hot" glue for a reason. Be careful.

NAIL SET Nail sets come in different sizes to fit the heads of different sized finish nails. They are used to drive the head of the nail below the surface of the wood without damaging it. They are also called punches.

PENETRATING OIL Penetrating oil is very useful for removing nuts that are stuck or rusted tight. You squirt a little on the nut and the oil works its way along the threads, allowing you to get it started.

PIPE WRENCHES Pipe wrenches come in a variety of sizes from small to very large. They are used to grip pipes for turning or cutting, and the more pressure you use, the tighter the wrench grips (so large pipes won't slip while you're working on them). If you get into working with pipes you'll need two.

The GADGET Guru
Make-It-Easy
Tip #10

CHECKING IT OUT—YOU CAN RENT BEFORE YOU BUY

You can't say it too many times, "the right tool for the right job" is the key to success. But sometimes the right tool is expensive and maybe the job is one you're going to do only once—like drilling holes in a concrete wall to put up some shelves. Clearly you'll need a drill with a lot of oomph. There's a good alternative that doesn't involve bothering the tool wizard who lives down the street or shelling out good money for something that's going to sit in the corner—you can rent. Rental houses carry everything from sledge hammers to cement mixers. Their shelves are full of specialty power and hand tools that will make your job easier and faster.

THE KEY HERE IS NOT TO GET IN OVER YOUR HEAD.

Just make sure you know how to use what you're renting both in terms of safety and efficiency. Don't be afraid to ask questions and get a demonstration and detailed instructions on how the tool works. A good rental house is happy to help you learn to use the tool—they want you to come back. And sometimes the price of the rental can be applied to purchase if you decide you can't live without it. It's a win-win situation.

SOCKET WRENCH AND SOCKETS Socket drives consist of a single handle with a ratchetting mechanism which allows you to turn the handle without having to reset it on the nut you're trying to tighten or remove. It comes with a series of socket heads to fit a variety of nuts. A socket set is very handy for assembling anything that comes from the store in a kit, like a bicycle or a picnic table.

STAPLE GUN Staple guns drive large staples into almost anything with maximum force and minimum effort. They make working with fabric or screening a breeze. There are electric models available but a good hand-operated model will also do just fine.

STUD FINDER Stud finders, essentially small metal detectors, are real time savers if you're trying to hang something on a wall. You move them across the wall and they beep or flash (or both) when they detect metal. Every time I point one at Roker he grins.

PART THREE

Getting Down to Business— Repair and Maintenance Projects Made Easy

Like the man said, it's time to get your feet wet. By now you've become familiar with your home, learned a little about how it works and started to put together a basic tool kit. Based on what you saw when you took a look around the house, you've probably already got some ideas about things you'd like to do, and you're ready to go. So let's get started.

In the following chapters you'll find plenty of projects to tackle, and although they vary in the skills required, nothing in this book is beyond the range of a beginning do-it-yourselfer. When you're starting out, pick projects you know you can handle, and then as your skills and confidence grow move on to bigger things.

HOW TO BEGIN

The world is divided into two kinds of people, those who read directions and those who think people who read directions have no sense of adventure. If you're the adventurous type, I don't want to dampen your spirit, but you'll need to make a little adjustment in your thinking to become a successful and satisfied household guru. Why? Because the more prepared you are when you actually begin working on something,

Make-It-Easy Tip #11

LIKE THE BOY SCOUTS SAY—*BE PREPARED*

You've got enough on your mind when you make a trip to the hardware store or building center to pick up materials for a home project. There's no reason to make the job harder by not being prepared to shop. What might seem simple at home can get pretty complex when you're standing in the aisle of a hardware jungle looking at thousands of products that suddenly all look the same.

Here are some tips for solid shopping:
- Spend quality time studying the project you're about to tackle and make a detailed list of what you're going to need to complete the job. There's nothing more frustrating than reaching a critical point in a job only to find that the fixture doesn't fit or that you need five more screws than you thought—and the store is closing in five minutes.
- An accurate tool and material list is important. But what's equally so is getting the exact replacement parts you need to repair something. There's an easy way to make sure you get what you need—**BRING THE BROKEN PARTS ALONG WHEN YOU GO TO THE STORE.** You can either match them yourself or show them to the hardware person and say, "I need one of these and one of those" (and you don't have to worry about what they're called).
- Although it's getting harder to find a store that stocks loose hardware in bins for single sale as well as complete replacement kits, see if you can find one. The reason? Why buy 13 screws prepackaged when you only need six? It's irritating to have to buy a complete replacement kit to get the one part you need. On the other hand, if you do need to replace everything, it's nice to know you can get it.

the greater success you'll have. One of the oldest rules in carpentry is **MEASURE TWICE, CUT ONCE**.

What good preparation does is help you get through the inevitable moments when things aren't exactly going your way. There's an element of the unexpected in every repair and maintenance job. Nuts might not loosen easily, or something might need a little adjustment to fit. But the more you know about how something's supposed to work, the easier the problems are to solve.

REMEMBER TO BE PATIENT AND DON'T BE AFRAID TO ASK—USE ONE OF THOSE 800 NUMBERS OR TALK TO THE PERSON AT THE HARDWARE STORE IF YOU'RE STUCK.

Professionals became skilled the same way you will: they asked questions and were willing to get their feet wet. If you follow your plan and are patient, thorough and careful, you'll get the job done right every time.

THE GADGET GURU'S ORDER OF BATTLE

1. See the problem.

2. Decide if it's something you can handle.

3. Break the project down into a step-by-step-by-step order.

4. Make lists of the tools and materials you're going to need and get everything in place and ready to go.

5. Give yourself plenty of time to complete the project. In other words, don't decide to rewire the dining room lamp half an hour before your dinner guests arrive.

6. Go over each step of the process in your mind before you begin and when you're ready...**go to work.**

CHAPTER SIX

Going with the Flow— **Plumbing**

The key to repairing and replacing plumbing fixtures is patience. And the most important thing to remember is that the hardest part of any plumbing job can be removing the old parts. Once you've done that, installation of the new one is pretty easy. All of the projects that follow are well within the range of beginners. I know because I've attempted and succeeded with all of them myself. And if I can do it so can you.

The skills you'll learn while doing these basic projects will soon allow you to tackle more difficult repairs and replacements and you'll be on your way to becoming a seasoned household repair pro. Let's get going with some simple and confidence building repairs.

TOOLS OF THE TRADE—**Plumbing**

• Tools You'll Use from Your Basic Kit

Adjustable Wrench	Pipe Wrenches	Tape Measure
Allen Wrenches	Plunger	Torpedo Level
Channel Lock Pliers	Putty Knife	Utility Knife
Cold Chisel	Screwdrivers	
Hacksaw	Snake	

MORE TOOLS OF THE TRADE

Here are some specialty plumbing tools you'll want to consider adding to your collection that will simplify most home plumbing repairs.

BALL PEEN HAMMER A hammer made especially for hitting metal.

BASIN WRENCH A special wrench for getting to faucet nuts underneath sinks.

SEAT DRESSING TOOL Used to resurface worn valve seats in compression faucets (can be rented).

SEAT WRENCH A special wrench for replacing or removing valve seats in compression faucets.

SMALL WIRE BRUSH Used for cleaning grit off pipes but also used for cleaning out drain traps.

SPUD WRENCH A special wrench for very large nuts such as those found on sink drains.

THE GADGET GURU'S STEP-BY-STEP GUIDE TO SOLVING COMMON PLUMBING PROBLEMS

DRAINS AND TRAPS—FIXING CLOGS AND LEAKS

MAKE-IT-EASY PROJECT #6-1
Clearing a Stopped Up Kitchen Sink with a Plunger

I'm a big believer in trying the easiest thing first, and when it comes to clogs there's nothing easier than starting with the trusty plumber's helper.

Level: Beginner
Tools: Plumber's helper

1) Take out the drain plug and/or strainer. Place the plunger over the drain opening and run cold water until it covers the plunger cup. This helps create the necessary vacuum. Move the plunger up and down rapidly and with short even strokes. It might take a while so don't give up too soon. If that doesn't work, then try what follows.

MAKE-IT-EASY PROJECT #6-2
Unclogging a Sink Trap Drain

Sometimes what stops up a drain is debris in the trap that hasn't made its way to the line. The trap is the first thing you pull apart when going after a clog.

Level: Beginner
Tools: Channel lock pliers * Wire brush
Also: Plastic bucket * Rubber gloves (optional) * An old towel (to put under the bucket; it saves on cleanup)

1) Put the bucket under the trap to catch the water and whatever else it's holding. Loosen the slip nuts with channel lock pliers. When they are loose they will slide away from the connections.

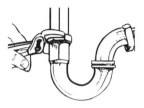

2) Pull the trap from the connections and dump it into the bucket. Use the wire brush to clean out any sticking debris. If necessary, take the trap to another sink and flush it with hot water. Reassemble and run water to check for leaks.

Make-It-Easy Tip #12

A WORD TO THE WISE—THE BEST REASON OF ALL NOT TO USE CAUSTIC DRAIN CLEANERS

If your drain is really clogged no drain cleaner, caustic or otherwise, will free it. That leaves one alternative. You or somebody else is going to have to remove the sink trap to work on it. What's the problem? The trap is going to be full of drain cleaner just waiting to spill out when you take the trap apart.

And believe me that stuff burns. For the record, the use of liquid cleaners more often than not can be considered a temporary, not permanent fix.

MAKE-IT-EASY PROJECT #6-3
Unclogging a Drain Line

If the trap is clear this is what you do next.

Level: Beginner to intermediate
Tools: Channel locks * Hand snake
Also: Bucket * Rubber gloves (optional)

1) Remove the trap. If there is a connecting pipe that goes into the wall remove it as well. Release a short length of coil from the hand snake and push the end into the opening until you feel it stop. This is the point where the pipe bends and goes down. Give yourself several inches of coil and lock it by tightening the set screw at the nozzle. Push the coil forward until it passes the bend. (Check manufacturer's instructions for specific details about operation.)

2) Untighten the set screw and start advancing the coil until it stops or advances slowly. This is likely to be whatever is clogging the pipe. Tighten the set screw and begin to crank the handle clockwise. If it's hair or some other solid object you can often grab it and pull it out by releasing the set screw and turning the crank.

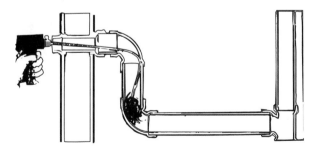

3) If the obstruction is accumulated soap or grease your mission is to bore through it several times to loosen and remove the buildup. Reconnect the lines and flush with hot water to send remaining waste matter on its way to the drain.

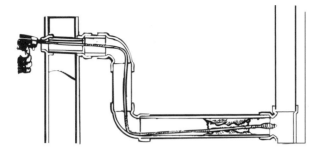

If you don't find obstructions in the trap or fixture line the clog is in one of the branch drains or the main stack. The next step is to call your plumber.

MAKE-IT-EASY PROJECT #6-4
Stopping the Leak in a Sink Strainer

Your sink strainer is the connection between the sink and the drain. It's got a lot of parts, and leaks can occur anywhere along the line.

Level: Beginner to intermediate
Tools: Channel lock pliers * Putty knife
            * Spud wrench
Materials: Plumber's putty * Replacement
            strainer kit or new washers and gas-
            kets

1) Use the channel locks to remove the slip nuts at the strainer connection and at the trap. Remove the connecting pipe (called the tailpiece).

2) Remove the lock nut with a spud wrench. If the lock nut is frozen, gentle tapping on the lugs (counterclockwise) will help loosen it. Remove the gaskets and washers and put them aside in the order they came off.

3) Lift the strainer out of the drain hole.

You'll see a ring of plumber's putty. Use the putty knife to scrape it off. If you are simply replacing the old strainer remove the putty from it as well.

NOTE: At this point you may have to stop work and make a trip to the hardware store to get replacement washers and gaskets or a replacement kit. If so, remember to take the old parts along so you can match them up. At the very least you should replace the old washers and gaskets while you've got the unit apart.

4) Apply a bead of plumber's putty around the lip of the drain opening. You don't have to go nuts but make sure there's enough to get a good seal. Press the strainer firmly into place.

5) Dive back under the sink and put the rubber washer and the rest of the rings back on in the order they came off. Screw on the lock nut and tighten with the spud wrench. Reconnect the tailpiece to the strainer and the trap and test for leaks.

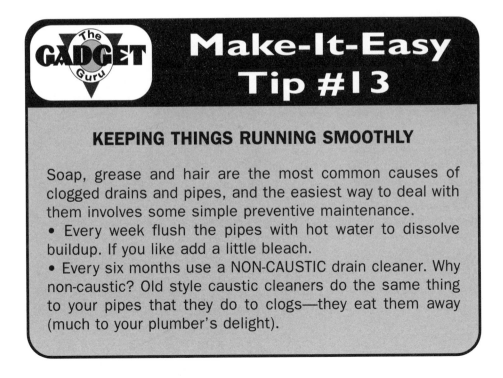

Make-It-Easy Tip #13

KEEPING THINGS RUNNING SMOOTHLY

Soap, grease and hair are the most common causes of clogged drains and pipes, and the easiest way to deal with them involves some simple preventive maintenance.

• Every week flush the pipes with hot water to dissolve buildup. If you like add a little bleach.

• Every six months use a NON-CAUSTIC drain cleaner. Why non-caustic? Old style caustic cleaners do the same thing to your pipes that they do to clogs—they eat them away (much to your plumber's delight).

CONTROLLING THE FLOW—
WORKING WITH FAUCETS

FAUCET BASICS

With a little patience and the right tools (nothing fancy) I believe almost anyone can repair or replace a faucet. The hardest part of the job is usually removing the old unit but once that's out of the way the rest is pretty simple.

Beneath Your Sink

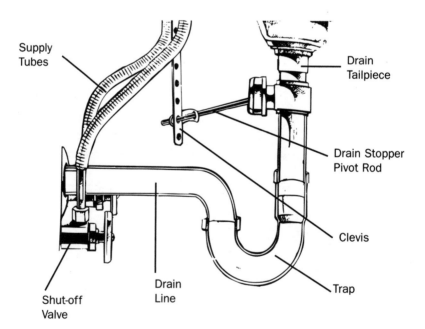

Supply Tubes

Drain Tailpiece

Drain Stopper Pivot Rod

Clevis

Trap

Drain Line

Shut-off Valve

There are four basic faucet designs: cartridge, ball-type, ceramic disc and compression (which is the oldest). You might have one or all of them in your house. Faucets that combine the handles and spout into one unit are referred to as "center set" faucets.

Here's what the most common faucets look like and how they work.

CARTRIDGE A sliding shaft or stem in a stationary sleeve that controls water on and water off with a push/pull motion. It controls water temperature by turning from side to side. Fixing a cartridge faucet is a one-piece replacement.

BALL–TYPE A hollow metal or plastic ball with holes is attached to the handle. The flow of hot and cold water is controlled by two valve seats and springs. The volume and temperature of the water is controlled by the position of the ball.

CERAMIC DISC Also a single handle faucet. Rotating the handle back and forth provides movement of one disc against the other controlling the flow and temperature.

MAYBE IT'S THE AERATOR

The aerator assembly screws onto the end of your faucet and catches tiny debris (non-harmful) and helps freshen the water. If water pressure seems low or the stream of water is uneven it's time to clean it out. Tape the jaws of a pair of pliers so you don't damage the fixture and unscrew it from the faucet, remove all the parts and note the order they go back together in. Clean off any deposits by soaking overnight in a lime dissolving solution (vinegar works very well). But before you spend time taking the old piece apart and cleaning it you should be aware that a new one costs about a buck so it might be simpler just to replace it.

COMPRESSION The flow of water is controlled by a rubber washer or disc that is mounted on a threaded stem which rotates up (water on) and down (water off). If you have separate hot and cold taps it's likely that your faucets are compression type.

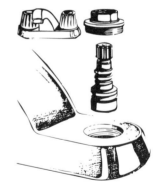

A FAUCET REPLACEMENT PRELIMINARY CHECKLIST

1. Look under the sink and find out the number of mounting holes in the sink ledge. Also check the distance between the center of each hole. It's usually 4 or 8 inches and is referred to as 4 or 8 inches *on center*. The narrower the distance the more difficult the installation because you have to work in a more confined space.

2. Make notes about how the connectors and water supply lines feed the existing faucet. Water supply lines come in several lengths so you need to measure the distance from the faucet to the shut-off valve. Leave some extra and be sure to match the fittings to the faucet and shut-off valve if the existing ones need to be replaced.

3. Decide whether you're going to replace or repair the existing unit.

MAKE-IT-EASY PROJECT #6-5
Replacing an Existing Kitchen or Bathroom Faucet

Dripping faucets are a real pain in the neck and one of the most annoying sounds around the house. Also annoying are leaks from the base of the faucet. They're easy to fix and most often the entire unit doesn't have to be replaced.

Level: Beginner
Tools: Phillips and regular screwdrivers * Adjustable wrench * Basin wrench * Pliers * Flashlight
Materials: New faucet * Teflon tape * Plumber's putty (on some installations) * Water supply lines and connectors (per faucet installation instructions)

Also: Penetrating oil (to help loosen corroded mounting nuts) *
            Hacksaw (if new supply lines need to be cut)

1) Turn off the water to both the
hot and cold supply lines and
then turn on the faucet to relieve
pressure. Once the pressure is
relieved the faucet should be
turned back off.

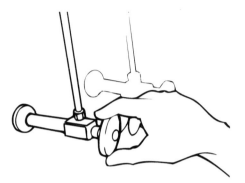

2) Disconnect the water supply
lines.

3) Remove the mounting nuts.
This is where you may need a
basin wrench, since getting to the
back of the sink can sometimes be
difficult.

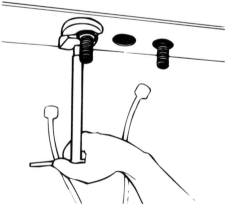

4) Remove the old faucet from the sink.

5) Clean the sink area. Remove old putty, if any.

6) Place new faucet in the holes.

7) Tighten the mounting nuts using the basin wrench if necessary.

8) Wrap the Teflon tape around the faucet inlet threads in a clockwise direction.

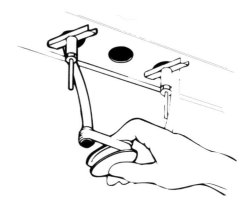

9) Tighten the supply line connections.

10) Turn the supply lines on and check all areas for leaks. Tighten nuts as necessary.

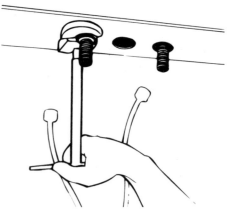

MAKE-IT-EASY PROJECT #6-6
Repairing or Replacing a Cartridge Faucet

Cartridge faucets come in kits with detailed instructions from the manufacturer. You'll need to know the make and model of your faucet when you go shopping. Generally the process is something very similar to this.

Level: Beginner
Tools: Screwdriver * Channel locks * Utility knife
Materials: Parts that come with the repair or replacement kit

1) Turn off the water supply valves below the sink.

2) Pop off the index cap on top of the faucet and remove the screw underneath.

3) Remove the handle by lifting up
and back.

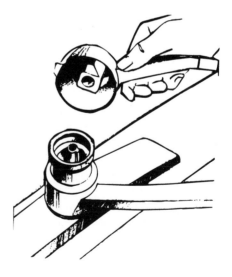

4) Use your channel locks to remove the retaining ring. You may find a retaining clip on some models. Remove this as well.

5) Note how the cartridge is aligned and again use the channel locks to pull it out. Put the new cartridge in the hole and align it the same way the old one was aligned.

6) Remove the spout by pulling up and twisting. You'll find rubber O-rings. Cut them off with a utility knife. Rub heat proof grease on the new rings and roll them down the stem until they slip into their grooves.

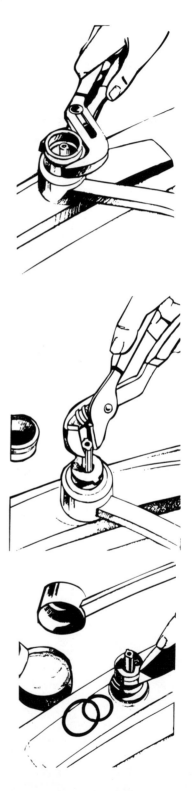

7) Reassemble the faucet in the reverse order of how it came apart. Turn on the supply valves, check for leaks, put away your tools and wash your hands or the dishes.

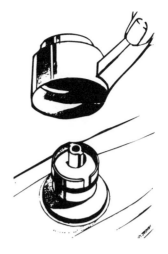

MAKE-IT-EASY PROJECT #6-7
Repairing or Replacing a Rotating Ball Faucet

Ball faucet repair and replacement kits also come with instructions and a special tool for loosening the faucet cam.

Level: Beginner
Tools: Channel locks * Slotted screwdriver
Materials: Parts that come with the replacement kit * Heat proof grease

1) You already know this, but be sure to turn off the water.

2) Find the set screw in the faucet handle and remove it.

3) Wrap the jaws of your channel locks with tape so you don't scratch the faucet cap and take it off.

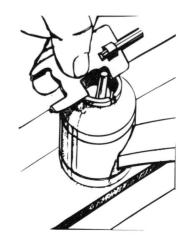

4) Use the cam tool that came with the replacement faucet to loosen the cam.

5) Remove the cam, its washer and the rotating ball. Make sure the ball isn't worn or damaged.

6) You'll see some springs and neoprene valve seats. Use a slotted screwdriver to remove them. Take off the spout.

7) Replace the O-rings on the spout stem. Remember to coat them with heat proof grease. Replace the spout. Install replacement springs and seats.

8) Reassemble the faucet, turn on the water and check for leaks.

MAKE-IT-EASY PROJECT #6-8
Repairing a Ceramic Disc Faucet

Before you replace a leaking ceramic assembly it's worth your time to try removing the seals and cleaning the unit.

Level: Beginner
Tools: Screwdriver
Materials: Parts that come with the repair or replacement kit

1) Shut off the supply valves under the sink.

2) Examine the handle of the faucet. Somewhere on it you will find a set screw that holds the handle in place. Remove the screw and lift off the handle.

3) Remove the escutcheon cap to reveal the disc assembly. You will probably see three screws. Remove them and lift out the cylinder.

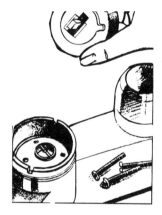

4) On the underside of the cylinder you'll find three neoprene seals. Pop them out carefully with a screwdriver and set them aside.

5) Clean the cylinder openings with a sponge or plastic scouring pad and rinse in warm water. Grit in the disc is a common cause of leaks.

6) Put the seals back in and put the faucet back together. Turn on the water with the faucet open. When the water is running through from the supply lines turn the faucet off. Turn it on again and check for leaks. If they continue you'll have to replace the entire cylinder with a new one.

MAKE-IT-EASY PROJECT #6-9
Repairing a Compression Faucet
(Replacing Washers, Valve Seats
and Resurfacing Valve Seats)

Level: Beginner
Tools: Flashlight * Phillips and slotted screwdrivers * Utility knife
            * Channel locks
Also: Seat wrench * Seat dressing tool (some rental houses carry
            seat dressing tools if you don't want to buy one)
Materials: Rubber washers * O-rings * Heat proof grease

NOTE: You can get kits of assorted sized washers and O-rings at the hardware store.

REPLACING WASHERS

1) Turn off the supply valves under the sink.

2) Pop off the cap on top of the faucet handle. Underneath you'll find a Phillips screw. Remove the screw and pull off the handle. The handle may be a little tight but it will come off.

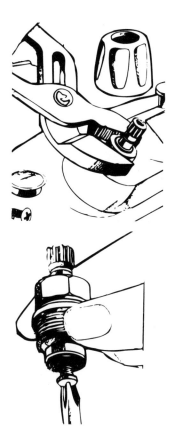

3) Use the channel locks to unscrew the stem and pull it out. If the stem is badly worn it should be replaced. At this point use your finger and a flashlight to inspect the valve seat. If it's smooth you're in good shape but if it feels rough it needs to be resurfaced. We'll get to that after you finish repairing the stem assembly.

4) Remove the stem washer by taking out the screw on the bottom.

5) Remove the spindle from the retaining nut.

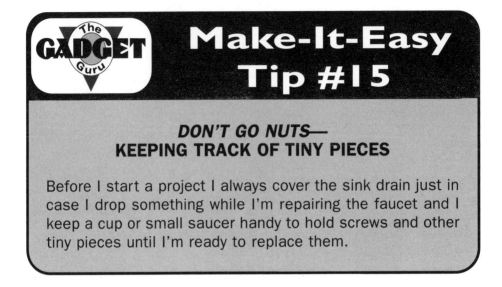

DON'T GO NUTS—
KEEPING TRACK OF TINY PIECES

Before I start a project I always cover the sink drain just in case I drop something while I'm repairing the faucet and I keep a cup or small saucer handy to hold screws and other tiny pieces until I'm ready to replace them.

6) Use the utility knife to cut off the old O-ring and replace it with an exact match. Replace the stem washer and put everything back together.

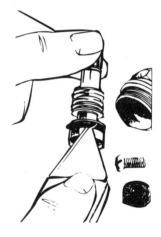

If the faucet still leaks, the seat valve is the culprit and needs to be resurfaced or replaced.

REPLACING VALVE SEATS

NOTE: Some valve seats are part of the faucet base and cannot be removed. We'll go through resurfacing a valve seat in the next segment.

1) Take a seat wrench, insert it into the valve and turn it counterclockwise to remove the seat. Match the valve seat exactly, rub the threads with heat proof grease and screw it into the valve.

2) Reassemble the faucet.

RESURFACING VALVE SEATS

1) The seat dressing has different sized cutting heads depending on the inside diameter of the valve. Select the proper one. Then slide the retaining nut over the shaft of the seat dressing tool.

2) Screw the retaining nut loosely into the valve body. Using a light touch turn the dressing tool clockwise two or three times. Inspect the seat again with your finger and flashlight. It should be smooth. If you can see or feel deep nicks, the faucet can't be successfully resurfaced and the unit will have to be replaced.

TAKING CARE OF THE FAMILY THRONE— *WORKING WITH TOILETS*

More than half the water that flows in and out of your home goes through your toilet and that's assuming it's in perfect working order. If it leaks or runs you're wasting thousands of gallons a year and adding significantly to your water bill. And I might mention that water damage to floors and ceilings from persistent leaks is another potentially serious drain on your bank account.

Toilets are so mechanically simple it's just plain silly not to learn the basics of maintaining and repairing them. All the working parts are in the tank, and the best way to see it in action is to lift the lid, flush it and watch the action.

INSIDE YOUR TOILET

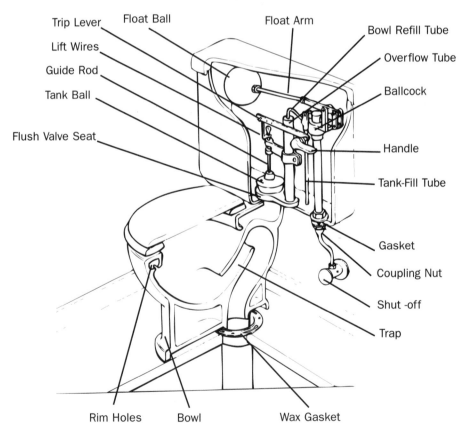

Trip Lever
Float Ball
Float Arm
Bowl Refill Tube
Lift Wires
Overflow Tube
Guide Rod
Tank Ball
Ballcock
Flush Valve Seat
Handle
Tank-Fill Tube
Gasket
Coupling Nut
Shut -off
Trap
Rim Holes
Bowl
Wax Gasket

When you push the outside handle the lever inside lifts a tank ball or flapper out of the flush valve seat at the bottom of the tank. The flush valve seat is connected to the toilet bowl. As gravity forces the water from the tank into the bowl, waste water is flushed out into the drain. As the water level in the tank falls, the float ball drops with it, opening the ballcock valve which is connected to the water supply. Fresh water from the inlet pipe then refills the tank and bowl. This makes the float ball rise until the ballcock valve closes, shutting off the water. That's all there is to it: no plugs, no cords, no motors—just gravity in action.

The problem is that all this simplicity spends its life sitting in water so things corrode, disintegrate and otherwise wear out. The great thing about toilets is that there isn't a repair that can't be made by beginners if they exercise a little patience and make a good plan of action.

REPAIRING, ADJUSTING AND REPLACING THE WORKING PARTS OF YOUR TOILET

When running toilet water is keeping you awake the problem is almost always in the tank. Water is leaking either in or out. A number of repair and replacement options will stop the drain on your nerves and bank account. Replacement kits come with complete instructions.

MAKE-IT-EASY PROJECT #6-10
Simple Toilet Fixes

1. ADJUSTING THE FLOAT ARM

If water is over the top of the overflow pipe or if it's leaking through the handle, the water level in the tank is too high. Ideally it should be about an inch or so below the top of the overflow pipe. Bend the float arm gently so the float ball is below the overflow pipe. If the water level is too low, bend the float arm up. Some float arms have an adjusting knob, so loosen the knob, set the float ball and retighten.

2. REPLACE A CRACKED FLOAT BALL

It's also possible that the float ball is cracked and holding water. If that's the case grip the float arm with a pair of pliers and unscrew the damaged float ball. Replace it and adjust the water level.

MAKE-IT-EASY PROJECT #6-11
Unclogging a Toilet

Like death and taxes, clogged toilets are one of life's certainties. Besides all the expected ways of stopping up a toilet, kids, adults and smart pets can find ways to drop all manner of objects into the bowl. A lot of us have been guilty of flushing, hoping that sponge or toothbrush will just go away. Unless the stoppage is really serious or far out of reach you've got a good chance of clearing it with a plunger or removing it with a closet snake.

Level: Beginner
Tools: Plunger or closet snake

1) Place the plunger over the toilet hole. As with a sink make sure that water covers the rubber cup so that you can get good suction. Move the plunger rapidly up and down in short strokes. Don't give up for several minutes; patience is the key. But if all your best efforts can't free the object with a plunger, it's time for the closet snake.

2) Feeding the coil up past the toilet trap and down into the drain can be tricky. It'll take you a few tries to be sure you're at the clog and not just stuck in a pipe bend. When you can feel the object in question turn the snake clockwise to grab it. Keep turning as you pull it out. Turn firmly but don't overdo it; you can break the bowl and that's a bummer because you'll have to replace the whole thing. If you can't get it after a few tries, you or your plumber may have to remove the toilet to get into the drain. But with any luck the snake will do the job.

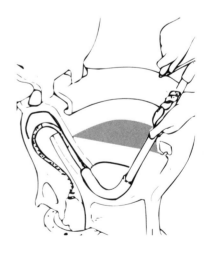

PUTTING ON A NEW TOILET SEAT

The majority of toilet seats these days come with plastic fittings, which make them very easy to put on. Problems can arise, however, when you're trying to take the old one off— especially if the fittings are metal or brass. Over the years the metal corrodes and the nuts might as well be welded to the threads. Even penetrating oil won't loosen them enough to screw them off.

What you can do is cut them off with your trusty hacksaw and you'll probably learn some new words while you're doing it.

Use plastic tape to protect the porcelain from mars and scratches, take the hacksaw and cut away. Work slowly using light to moderate pressure. Admit to yourself that it'll take a while, and be patient, you'll get the job done.

MAKE-IT-EASY PROJECT #6-12
Leaky Ballcocks

The ballcock is where the supply water comes into your toilet. It will eventually start to leak. The mechanism is inexpensive, and since you're going to the trouble of taking it apart you might as well replace the whole thing.

Level: Beginner
Tools: Adjustable wrench
Materials: New ballcock assembly

1) Shut off the water supply and flush to drain the tank. Unscrew the float arm from the ballcock. Remove the ballcock from the tank by

unhooking the supply line and unscrewing the mounting nut.

2) Put the washer on the ballcock per manufacturer's instructions and set it in the hole. Refit the supply line and tighten the mounting nut.

3) Clip or bend the refill tube so the tip is inside the overflow pipe.

4) Put the float arm back on (make sure it passes behind the overflow pipe). Turn on the water and adjust the float arm to set the water level.

MAKE-IT-EASY PROJECT #6-13
Repairing a Leaking Float Cup Unit

There are two kinds of float cup assemblies: one uses a tank ball and the other uses a flapper. Both are easy to replace.

Level: Beginner
Tools: Screwdriver
Materials: Replacement tank ball
             or flapper (if necessary)

1) Adjust the tank ball or flapper so it is directly over the flush valve. The tank ball has a guide arm that you can adjust with a screwdriver. The flapper is raised and lowered by a chain.

2) If the tank ball is damaged, unscrew it from the guide arm and replace it.

3) The flapper is attached to lugs on the overflow pipe and has a ring to catch the chain. Replace if necessary.

MAKE-IT-EASY PROJECT #6-14
Repairing a Leaky Toilet Tank

Eventually the connection between the bowl and the tank will begin to leak. It's just the way life is. While there are a lot of projects you can do on your own, there are times when you need an assistant.

Level: Beginner (with an assistant)
Tools: Slotted screwdriver * Adjustable wrench
Materials: Rubber replacement washers (if necessary)

1) Shut off the supply valve and flush the toilet to drain the tank.

2) Look in the bottom of the tank and find the bolts that hook the tank to the bowl.

3) Have your assistant use the screwdriver to hold the bolt inside the tank steady while you slowly and gently tighten the nut with the adjustable wrench. Dry everything off and turn on the supply valve. Flush the toilet and check for leaks. If it's still dripping you'll have to replace the rubber washers.

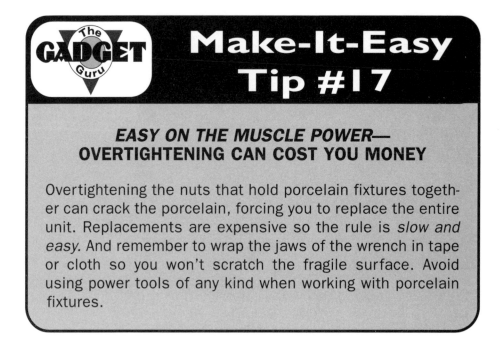

EASY ON THE MUSCLE POWER— OVERTIGHTENING CAN COST YOU MONEY

Overtightening the nuts that hold porcelain fixtures together can crack the porcelain, forcing you to replace the entire unit. Replacements are expensive so the rule is *slow and easy.* And remember to wrap the jaws of the wrench in tape or cloth so you won't scratch the fragile surface. Avoid using power tools of any kind when working with porcelain fixtures.

4) Drain the tank again. Remember, this is a process. Replace the rubber washers one side at a time so the tank doesn't shift position. Tighten gently but firmly. Test for leaks. If they're still there, the problem is in the flush valve.

MAKE-IT-EASY PROJECT #6-15
Replacing a Flush Valve Washer

This is actually two projects in one because you'll follow the same steps if you ever have to replace the tank. If you replace the tank, however, you'll need to install the inner workings.

Level: Beginner (with assistant)
Tools: Slotted screwdriver * Adjustable wrench * Spud wrench
Materials: Flush valve washer * Soft spud washer

1) Drain the tank by shutting off the supply valve and flushing the toilet. Disconnect the ballcock refill tube and take off the toilet tank by removing the bolts.

2) Remove the flush valve with the spud wrench. Note how the washers are placed on the flush valve and how the flush valve is set in the tank (see master illustration, p. 86).

3) Take the cone shaped washer and slide it onto the flush valve stem the same way the old one came off. Put the flush valve back into its hole in the tank.

4) Screw the spud nut back onto the flush valve and tighten. Put on the new soft stud washer, put the tank back on the bowl and rebolt it.

COMMON TOILET PROBLEMS AND SOLUTIONS

TOILET WON'T FLUSH

Check the handle, trip lever, guide arm, float arm, and the connections between the parts to make sure all are functioning. The handle may be too loose or tight, the trip lever or guide arm may be bent or broken or out of alignment, preventing the stopper ball from rising far enough.

The Gadget Guru

Make-It-Easy Tip #18

NO SWEAT—
STOPPING CONDENSATION ON A TOILET TANK

Line the tank with foam sheets specially made for the inside of toilet tanks to prevent condensation and sweating.

WATER RUNS, BUT TANK WON'T FILL PROPERLY

The handle and trip assembly may be malfunctioning. Check the stopper ball to make sure it's seated properly; check the flush valve seat to see if it's damaged or corroded. See if water has leaked into the float ball.

WATER CONTINUES TO RUN AFTER THE TANK IS FILLED

Try adjusting the float downward. Make sure the float isn't damaged and that it doesn't have water in it. See if the inlet valve washers are leaking. If so, replace them. Check to see that the stopper ball is seated properly. Check the flush seat valve for corrosion.

THE WATER LEVEL IS TOO HIGH OR TOO LOW

Carefully bend the float arm downward to lower the water level. Bend it upward to raise it. There is also an adjustment screw on the inlet valve. Ideally the water level should be about an inch below the top of the overflow tube.

TOILET WON'T FLUSH PROPERLY

Water level is probably too low in the tank. Bend the float ball arm up to allow more water to flow into the toilet bowl.

WATER SPLASHES IN THE TANK WHILE IT REFILLS

Adjust the refill tube that runs into the overflow tube. It may also be necessary to replace the washers in the inlet valve.

SPEND A LITTLE TIME IN THE SHOWER— BASIC MAINTENANCE

MAKE-IT-EASY PROJECT #6-16
Recaulking Your Bathtub or Shower

Your bathtub is heavy when it's empty and even heavier when it's full of water. But, no matter how rock solid it looks there's a lot of shifting and movement. You might never even know there's a leak in your bathtub until you find water dripping from the ceiling below it and pay a big bill for replacing rotted and water damaged flooring. Maintaining the seal around the bathtub is simple, inexpensive and guaranteed to save you money in the long run. Examine the seams of your tub or shower stall. If you see cracks or missing chunks it's time to go to work.

Level: Beginner
Tools: Carpenter's awl or can opener * Utility knife * Clean rags
Materials: Tub and tile silicone caulk (squeeze tube) * Rubbing alcohol

1) Use the can opener or awl to scrape the old material from the seams. Clean soap scum and mildew from the joints with a clean rag and rubbing alcohol. Take your time and do a thorough job because the new caulking won't set properly on a dirty surface.

2) Fill the tub with water so that the joint will expand to its maximum spacing. Cut off the tip of the caulking tube with a utility knife making an ⅛ inch opening. Start at one end and carefully run a bead for three feet or so along the seam. It's better to work in small segments.

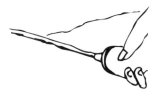

NOTE: Check with your hardware store because caulk is coming out in designer colors these days. Also, in case you are going to be doing a lot of caulking, electric caulking guns are now available. They might be worth a look.

3) Wet your finger and smooth the caulk into the seam. Proceed until all the joints are filled and neat. Once the caulk has dried completely use your utility knife to trim away any excess. Check the manufacturer's instructions for drying times but assume it's going to take at least 12 hours to set properly. It's important that the caulk is completely dry before you spend an hour in the shower or read the Sunday paper in the tub.

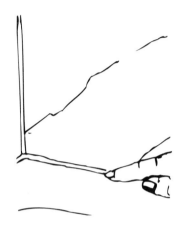

MAKE-IT-EASY PROJECT #6-17
Maintaining a Shower Head

It's very easy to replace a shower head, and if you want to get into something fancier than the one you've got, that's the way to go. But it's also very simple to clean the one that's already there.

Level: Beginner
Tools: Adjustable wrench * Paper clip or thin wire * Toothbrush
Materials: O-ring * Heat proof grease * Vinegar

1) Tape the jaws of the adjustable wrench so it won't scratch the surface, and unscrew the nut that attaches the shower head to the pipe.

2) Unbend the paper clip and clean the holes. If there are a lot of mineral deposits soak the head overnight in vinegar and use an old toothbrush to remove them. Rinse away debris with clean water.

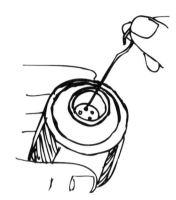

3) If the O-ring is worn replace it. Remember to rub it with heat proof grease before slipping it into place. Reinstall the shower head. Enjoy.

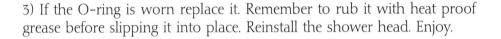

THE HEAT IS ON—
MAINTAINING YOUR WATER HEATER

MAKE-IT-EASY PROJECT #6-18
Removing Sediment from the Tank of Your Electric Water Heater

However pure your water source is, sediment is going to build up in your tank and eventually it's going to interfere with the heating element. When there's enough buildup the heating element will burn out and have to be replaced. There is no firm rule about how often the tank should be flushed, but in general, the harder the water in your area, the more often it should be done. It doesn't take a lot of time and it's a lot easier than replacing the element. Get some advice from your local plumbing supply or your local plumber.

Level: Beginner
Tools: Garden hose

1) Turn off the water heater, then the cold water supply valve. If you don't have a cold water valve you must shut off the main valve. Open the hot water faucets in the house to prevent air lock in the pipes.

2) Attach a garden hose to the drain cock on the water heater and run it outside or to the nearest floor drain. Open the drain cock and empty the tank.

3) When the tank is empty turn on the cold water supply and flush the tank until the water is clear and free of sediment. Shut off the drain cock and fill the tank with cold water. You'll know it's full when the faucet upstairs is running. Turn the faucet off, shut off the drain cock, turn on the supply valve or main and turn on the water heater.

MAKE-IT-EASY PROJECT #6-19
Replacing a Leaky Relief Valve on a Water Heater

The relief valve is located on top of the water heater and prevents the heater from exploding if the thermostat fails and the water gets too hot. When it begins to release pressure constantly it's time to replace it.

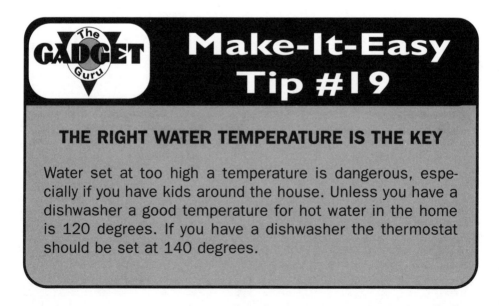

GADGET The Guru   Make-It-Easy Tip #19

THE RIGHT WATER TEMPERATURE IS THE KEY

Water set at too high a temperature is dangerous, especially if you have kids around the house. Unless you have a dishwasher a good temperature for hot water in the home is 120 degrees. If you have a dishwasher the thermostat should be set at 140 degrees.

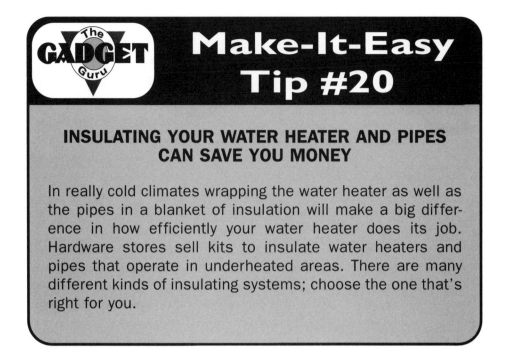

Make-It-Easy Tip #20

INSULATING YOUR WATER HEATER AND PIPES CAN SAVE YOU MONEY

In really cold climates wrapping the water heater as well as the pipes in a blanket of insulation will make a big difference in how efficiently your water heater does its job. Hardware stores sell kits to insulate water heaters and pipes that operate in underheated areas. There are many different kinds of insulating systems; choose the one that's right for you.

Level: Beginner
Tools: Adjustable wrench
Materials: Replacement relief valve * Plumber's joint compound

1) Turn off the water heater and the cold water supply valve. I suggest waiting for the water in the tank to cool down or using this opportunity to flush the tank. Remove the valve. Get an exact replacement.

2) Apply some plumber's pipe joint compound to the threads and screw it back into place.

Make-It-Easy Tip #21

IF YOU NEED TO DRAIN YOUR PLUMBING SYSTEM

If you're going to be out of town for a few weeks on vacation and you want to shut off the water, you can turn off the house main in the basement. But if you've had a major plumbing emergency of any kind and the plumber will be replacing main feed pipes, you can save a little time draining the system yourself. Also, if a major renovation requires new plumbing, the system might have to be drained. Both the house main (yours) and the street main will have to be shut down. Here's how to drain your system so you won't blow out your pipes when you turn it back on:

- Shut off the street main first, then the house main.
- After you've closed both valves, take a bucket and your adjustable wrench and slowly loosen the union nut on the house side of the meter until water that has accumulated there drains out. Meanwhile move around the house and open all faucets to drain the water in the pipes. Once all the faucets are open go back into the basement and slowly open the house main and drain any water that remains in the meter into your bucket. When all the water is gone, retighten the meter union nut on the house side, just so you don't forget.
- When you're ready to turn the water back on, check to make sure all the faucets are open so air can bleed out of the pipes as they refill with water. Open the meter valves (street first) partway and run until all the air has escaped through the faucets and water is flowing smoothly.
- Turn off the faucets and open the meter valves all the way. There will likely be some small bursts of air when the faucets are first turned on after full pressure is restored, but this is normal and nothing to worry about.

CHAPTER SEVEN

Current Issues—
What You Need to Know
about Electricity

Unlike a lot of other home projects most electrical work is done indoors where it's warm and cozy and your hands don't get very dirty. Personally, I think that's reason enough to tackle an electrical project. But let's face it, most of us are scared to death to make electrical repairs. In order to put your fears to rest, remember this simple point: electricity cannot hurt us unless it is turned on. Really!

Make-It-Easy Tip #22

FIRST THINGS FIRST—GO TO THE SOURCE

If you flick a switch and nothing happens, the first thing to do is check the light bulb before you tear the electrical system apart. Sometimes it's just loose in the socket and a little jiggling will restore the power.

It's useful in the beginning to compare the electrical and plumbing systems in your home in order to get a picture of how the electrical system works—but there's one big difference. If you forget to turn off the water supply to work on a faucet you get wet, but if you forget to turn off the electricity before you replace a switch you get zapped. Needless to say, the potential consequences are very serious. An electrical shock can not only injure you, but kill you.

So, I ask myself a simple question every time I get ready to go on an electrical project.

"DID YOU TURN OFF THE POWER, DUMMY?"

The answer has always been yes, but I always ask the question anyway. And I am not hesitant to double check to make sure it is turned off before starting a project. Poor old electricity isn't the cause of accidents—carelessness is. Solid preparation and knowing what the potential hazards are allow you to take care of a lot of electrical business and really save some money. It's just common sense—don't jump into something you haven't thought through and don't fully understand.

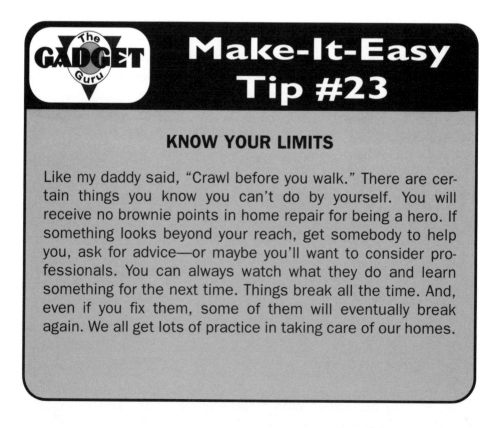

Make-It-Easy Tip #23

KNOW YOUR LIMITS

Like my daddy said, "Crawl before you walk." There are certain things you know you can't do by yourself. You will receive no brownie points in home repair for being a hero. If something looks beyond your reach, get somebody to help you, ask for advice—or maybe you'll want to consider professionals. You can always watch what they do and learn something for the next time. Things break all the time. And, even if you fix them, some of them will eventually break again. We all get lots of practice in taking care of our homes.

Make-It-Easy Tip #24

SAFETY FIRST: COMMON ELECTRICAL SENSE

• Always shut down the power to the circuit you're going to work on at the main service panel. Each circuit should be labeled clearly so you know exactly what you're switching on and off. It doesn't even hurt to throw a piece of tape over the breaker so that another family member won't accidentally turn it on while you are working.

• Learn to use your circuit tester and continuity tester (see p. 48 and p. 49) to make sure there aren't any surprises.

• Unplug any appliance or fixture before you begin work.

• Replace damaged plugs and frayed or damaged cords immediately.

• Don't use any electrical appliances in the bathtub, and whenever you're handling any electrical equipment don't touch radiators or faucets at the same time. Your electrical system is likely to be grounded to the plumbing system, and if something's wrong you could get zapped.

• When you use an adapter to make a three-prong plug fit into a two prong receptacle, make sure you take the little green grounding wire and hook it to the screw in the receptacle plate.

• If a fuse blows regularly don't replace it with another one of higher amperage. Take the time to find out why it's blowing instead. (See Make-It-Easy Project #7-9.)

• When you remove a plug from the wall, don't pull it out by the cord. It loosens the connections and creates a potential fire hazard.

• No matter how convenient it seems, don't run extension cords under carpets or rugs. If the cord frays, you've got trouble and you probably won't find out about it until it's too late.

• Use a properly rated extension cord for whatever you do.

• Wear rubber boots if you're doing electrical work on a damp floor.

What I want to make clear is that by following some common sense rules of safety a beginner can do simple electrical replacement and repair with a sense of security and confidence.

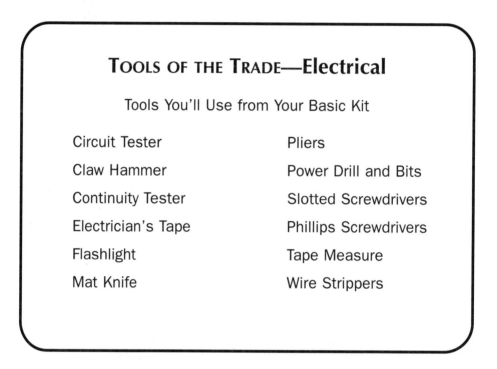

TOOLS OF THE TRADE—Electrical

Tools You'll Use from Your Basic Kit

Circuit Tester	Pliers
Claw Hammer	Power Drill and Bits
Continuity Tester	Slotted Screwdrivers
Electrician's Tape	Phillips Screwdrivers
Flashlight	Tape Measure
Mat Knife	Wire Strippers

MORE TOOLS OF THE TRADE

Here are some specialty electrical tools you'll want to consider adding to your collection on a project-by-project basis.

LINEMAN'S PLIERS These pliers, also called electrician's pliers, are used for cutting cable and twisting wire to make connections. They are heavy duty but they're the right tool for electrical work.

Make-It-Easy Tip #25

GET YOURSELF A TOOL BELT

A tool belt that holds the hardware and tools you need to do a project frees your hands and keeps everything organized and close by. Not only is it macho (you should see what I look like wearing mine), but it's a safety factor as well. Accidents can happen while you're reaching for a faraway tool or dropping something from a ladder.

The hardware outlets have entire sections devoted to tool belts. There's a huge selection so I'm sure you can find the one that suits (and fits) you. It'll be useful in every area of home repair.

NEEDLE NOSE PLIERS
Needle nose pliers are small and pointed at the end. They're perfect for getting into tight places and bending and shaping wire.

MAKE-IT-EASY PROJECT #7-1
Be Like Columbus—Chart the Circuits in Your Home

This is the very first thing you should do before starting in on electrical repair and maintenance projects. The time spent now will speed up any work you do later and help you feel secure and confident when you begin a project.

Level: Beginner
Tools: Pencil and paper * Black waterproof marker
Materials: White tape (the kind you can write on)
Also: An assistant to help flip switches around the house

AN ELECTRICAL PROJECT CHECKLIST

Here are some tips that will help make you a successful household electrician.

• Have a plan in place. Imagine what needs to be done and go through it step by step.

• Ask yourself my favorite question. If you've forgotten, it's "DID YOU TURN OFF THE POWER, DUMMY?"

• Before you remove the unit look at how it was installed and remember it. Making a sketch can help avoid confusion and mistakes later. This is also a good use for that Polaroid collecting dust in the closet. And don't throw away the instructions when you open the box—they are there for a reason.

• Have something available to hold any loose screws or parts so you don't have to search for them later.

• Be a packrat. Save the screws and other loose parts from pieces you've replaced. It's what the pros do and you'll be surprised how handy it is to have a few spare parts lying around.

• Make sure you're using an exact replacement—unless you're upgrading. In that case make sure the upgrade will work where you want to put it. Take the old piece with you to the hardware store when you go shopping. All electrical hardware is rated and approved for specific use. Don't put a square peg in a round hole.

• Buy only electrical parts (like switches and plugs) that have the Underwriter's Laboratory (UL) stamp of approval. They've been thoroughly tested and will do what they're supposed to.

1) Draw a simple floorplan of your home that shows all the outlets and appliances. Number each outlet or appliance on the map.

2) Plug a lamp or a radio into each outlet and turn all the switches on.

3) Set yourself up at the breaker panel and have your assistant upstairs ready to go. One by one start flipping the breakers. Have your assistant move through the house and call out which outlet, switch or appliance goes off when you hit a breaker.

4) Note the circuit breaker number in the appropriate place on the map and put the outlet information on a label next to its breaker.

5) Continue until all the breakers are accounted for. You'll probably find you have some spare breakers; label them too. Put a copy of the map in a plastic sleeve or envelope and hang it up next to the circuit breaker panel. Put another copy in your general house file.

MAKE-IT-EASY PROJECT #7-2
Learning to Use a Circuit Tester and a Continuity Tester

This project is another kind of learning step. Learning how to use the continuity tester and the circuit tester not only is important for your safety but can tell you a lot about what's going on electrically.

USING A CIRCUIT TESTER

The circuit tester tells you if current is running through a circuit—in other words it tells you if the power is on or off. Read and follow the instructions that come with the tester. This is one of your most important electrical tools.

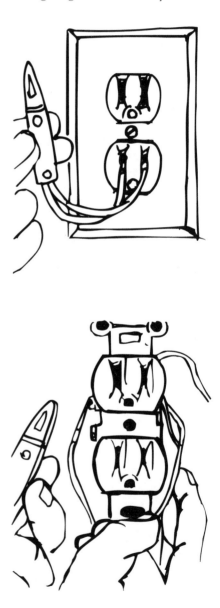

TESTING A GROUNDED OUTLET

It's a two step process and both are important.

• The first step in testing an outlet is to stick the two little prongs into each slot of the receptacle. If the light goes on, there is power. Go to the circuit breaker panel and shut off the breaker. Then proceed to the next step.

• Remove the cover plate of the outlet and then the mounting screws that hold the outlet in the **JUNCTION BOX.** (The junction box is the metal box mounted in the wall and holds the outlet securely in place.) Carefully remove the outlet without touching the wires or terminal screws. Touch one of the probes to a brass terminal and the other to the silver terminal on the other side. Test the terminals on both outlets. If the tester doesn't glow the circuit is off and you can proceed.

You can also use the tester to check if a three prong outlet is grounded. Place one probe in the narrower of the two slots (Hot) and the other in the grounding hole below. If the light doesn't come on, the outlet isn't grounded.

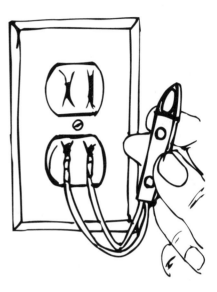

TESTING A TWO-SLOT OUTLET

With the power on, stick a probe into each slot. If it doesn't light up, the power is off. If it does, flip the breaker. To check whether or not the circuit is grounded, place a probe into the hot slot and touch the screw on the cover plate with the other. If the light goes on, the circuit is grounded. (Make sure there's no paint on the screw because you won't get a good contact if there is.)

TESTING A SWITCH

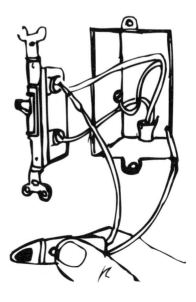

In order to test a switch you have to remove it from the junction box.
• Take off the cover plate and remove the mounting screws and pull out the switch without touching the terminals or wires.
• Touch one of the probes to a terminal and the other to the junction

box. The light should stay off. Test the other terminal. If the light stays off, you're in business. If it glows, then you've got power and need to flip the circuit breaker before you begin to work.

USING A CONTINUITY TESTER

The continuity tester tells you if a switch, receptacle or fixture is faulty. It's another big league electrical tool. Make it your friend.

To try it out, attach the alligator clip to a terminal on an outlet and touch the probe to the terminal on the other side. If the light in the tester goes on, the outlet is in working order. If it doesn't, the outlet is faulty and must be replaced. Take a look at the manual that came with the continuity tester for more ways to use it when you're testing electrical equipment.

MAKE-IT-EASY PROJECT #7-3
Replacing Plugs and Making
Extension Cords

Putting a new plug on the end of a piece of wire is so simple it's silly. And it's a great way to build a skill and confidence level with electrical tools. Most of the tools you'll use for electrical repairs are used to fix plugs and cords—clippers, wire cutters, cable strippers, and screwdrivers. Consider this project a learning experience.

Level: Beginner
Tools: Screwdriver * Wire stripper * Wire clippers
Materials: Plugs * Cable

1) Snip the old or damaged plug from the cable with the wire cutters.

2) If you're using a snap-on or clip-on plug, snap or clip it in place and you're done. (Snap-ons are easy to install but not as sturdy as the styles with screw terminals.) If the plug has screw terminals, proceed.

3) Use the wire strippers or a utility knife to strip the rubber sheathing back from the end of the cable about 2 inches. If you use a utility knife be careful not to cut the wires inside. **NOTE:** Household Zip cord is simply two pieces of wire molded side by side into plastic cable. It comes in several different gauges. Once you strip off the insulation layer you're ready to wire.

Make-It-Easy
Tip #27

THE WORLD OF PLUGS AND WIRE

Plugs come in a lot of different shapes and sizes. They range in complexity from simple snap-ons for regular Zip cords (standard lamp wire) to the three-prong "twist-lock" giants used for major appliances. But no matter how big or small, they all work in the same way—wire is connected to the prongs on the plug and the plug is inserted into an outlet.

Two prong plugs have a "hot" prong, which is the narrow one, and a "neutral" prong, which is the widest. If your plug has three prongs the third one is round and is the "ground."

You've got to use wire cable that's rated for the job it's going to do. If you try to run your window air conditioner on a regular household extension cord you'll find out why there are different types of wire for specific jobs. Eventually the cord will get so hot it'll melt and maybe burn. Remember resistance?

The next time you're in the hardware store look at the rolls of electrical cable. They come in several thicknesses or "gauges" and are rated in amps. Ironically, the lower the rating, the more current the cable can handle. The counter people can help you get the right size or "gauge" of wire and the right plug for the job you need it to do.

4) You might find a layer of material between the outer sheathing and the wires—if so cut that away as well. Note that you'll find either two or three wires. Black and white or black and white and green. Black is *hot*, white is *neutral* and green is the *ground*. Use the cable strippers to remove about ¾ inch of the insulation to expose the copper wire. The wire is either made of tiny strands wrapped together or a single piece. If the wire is stranded, twist the strands clockwise until tight.

5) Run the cable through the plug and tie what's called an "Underwriter's Knot" before you screw the wire to the terminals. (The knot will help relieve stress on the connections when the cord is jerked around.)

6) You'll see terminals that are brass and silver on the plug, each connected to the prongs. Screw the black, or *hot*, wire to the brass terminal and the white, or *neutral*, to the silver. Wrap the wires around the terminals in a clockwise direction and screw them into place. If the cable is grounded you'll attach the green *"ground"* wire to the third terminal. Replace the fiber disc that covers the wires in the plug.

To make an extension cord put a male plug on one end of the cable and a female on the other.

MAKE-IT-EASY PROJECT #7-4
Rewiring Lamps

Unless you really hate a lamp and are looking for a reason to get rid of it, there's no reason to send it to the Dumpster just because it's stopped working. Replacing the cord and socket is one of the simplest fix up projects on the planet. In fact it's so easy even Roker can do it. Sometimes it's just a matter of a little cleaning and maintenance. You might examine the fixture and discover that the plug is cracked—and you already know how to take care of that.

And somebody like Martha Stewart will be the first to tell you that knowing how to rewire a lamp opens the door to creating custom fixtures of your own. A great Saturday (after the *Today* show, of course) project is putting a shade on top of an interesting base, wiring it up and waiting for your friends to congratulate you on your taste, creativity and electrical skill. Being frugal has never been so much fun.

Level: Beginner
Tools: Slotted screwdriver * Wire cutters
Materials: Replacement socket * Replacement plug * Electrical lamp
            cord (often Zip cord) * Electrician's tape

1) Set up a working space on a table or counter. Remove the shade. Remove the harp (which is the curved brass wire that holds up the lamp shade) by squeezing it until it snaps out of the retaining sleeves.

GADGET The Guru

Make-It-Easy Tip #28

WIRE NUTS AND YOU

When you begin to do electrical projects you'll discover that sometimes you need to "splice" two wires together to make a connection. One way to do it is twist the two wires together in a clockwise direction, wrap each of them tightly in electrical tape and then tape them tightly to the body of the cable. This type of splice is used when the connection is permanent and the cable may be stressed. Get some advice on permanent splices from a professional or your friend at the hardware store.

The other way involves using what are called wire nuts. Wire nuts are insulated plastic caps that come in different sizes for different sizes of wire and essentially they screw onto the bare wires like a bottle cap. They're easy to use and very safe.

Remove about half an inch of insulation from the wires you are joining and twist them together in a clockwise direction (use a pair of pliers to get a good tight twist). Then screw the wire nut onto the connection until it's tight. Check that the connection is "made" by pulling easily on each wire and make sure that the cap covers any wire that is exposed.

Wire nuts are not designed for a connection that gets any stress.

2) On some lamps the harp goes onto the lamp before the socket. If that's the case jump ahead to step 6, removing the socket. But before you go any further check the contact tab in the base of the socket. If it's dirty or bent down the bulb won't make contact. Try cleaning it and gently prying it up with a screwdriver.

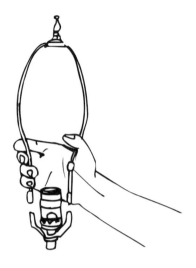

3) Remove the insulating sleeve and shell by squeezing on the sleeve where it says PRESS. That releases the sleeve and shell from the base of the socket.

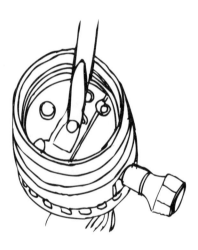

4) Now go to the bottom of the lamp. Remove the base cover (usually felt if there is one) carefully, so you can put it back later. Cut the old cable about a foot from the base of the lamp. Strip an inch or so of insulation from the old cord and from the cord you're going to replace it with. Twist the ends of old and new together and wrap them with a piece of electrician's tape.

5) Pull the new cord up through the base and out the top. Cut off the old cord and strip ¾ inch of insulation off the new one in preparation to make the connections. The cable will separate easily down the middle to give you as much slack as you need to work.

6) Unscrew the old socket cap from the lamp base and put the new one in place. Otherwise, you might wire the new socket before you screw in the new cap. (Nobody likes doing things twice—especially me.) Tie an Underwriter's Knot in the wires to relieve stress.

Make-It-Easy Tip #29

GETTING A BROKEN BULB OUT OF A SOCKET

Occasionally, in fact quite often, I've found that in some of my specialty fixtures like chandeliers, the bulb will burn out and is frozen in the socket. Sometimes I'll find that out after I've twisted the lamp right out of its base leaving the bulb in my hand and the base in the socket. This is where needle nose pliers really come in handy. Turn off the power to the fixture or unplug it. Use the needle nose pliers to grasp the filament and gently turn it counterclockwise. The base should begin to twist out. Turn until you can finish by hand.

If that doesn't work, spread the jaws of the pliers against the inside of the socket. This should give you enough leverage to begin twisting it out.

By the way, always turn off or unplug a fixture before you change the bulb—dummy! (Hey, I'm just trying to keep you safe so you can buy my next book!)

Make-It-Easy Tip #30

DON'T OVEREXTEND YOURSELF—
SAFE USE OF EXTENSION CORDS IS IMPORTANT

Improper use of extension cords is extremely dangerous. If you don't believe me, just ask your local fire department. A lot of fires in the home are caused by asking the electrical system to do things it can't. Modern electrical codes now require that outlets be placed in regular intervals along the walls so people won't be tempted to run too much extra cable.

This is all fine and dandy if you live in a new house.

But in older homes extension cords are a fact of life unless you go in for major rewiring. The bottom line is that the cord you're using has to be rated for the load it's carrying, especially if you're trying to run several things off a single cable. The problem is resistance. If the cord is rated at 15 amps and it's drawing 30 amps of current, eventually it'll get hot enough to burn. If the circuit breaker or fuse doesn't trip in time, you could be in for a fire.

This is not a good thing.

So the Gadget Guru says:

• Use extension cords only when you have to.
• Make sure they're beefy enough to carry the load.
• Keep them as short as possible.
• Check regularly for damage.

7) The copper wire in a lamp cord is comprised of strands. Twist the ends of these strands clockwise until they're tight. In standard lamp cord there is no designated *"hot"* or *"neutral"* wire because all you're doing is completing a circuit between the lamp socket and the plug, so you can use either one on either terminal. Form a hook in one wire, slide it on the

brass terminal clockwise and turn the terminal screw into place. Do the same with the other wire and put it on the silver terminal.

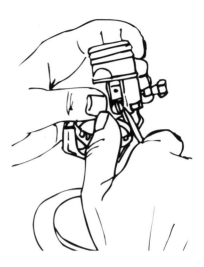

8) Once the wires are firmly in place, reassemble the socket and screw it back on the lamp. Replace the felt and put on a new plug. (See the section on making an extension cord, p. 110.) Just make sure you've left enough slack on the cord to reach the outlet of choice.

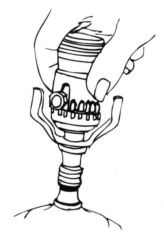

MAKE-IT-EASY PROJECT #7-5
Hooking Up Receptacles

There are two basic types of receptacles or outlets, side-wired, which have screw terminals on the side, and back-wired, which use "push-in" terminals instead of screws. Although you can change the style of the receptacle it must fit in the junction box and have the same rating as the old one. It does you no good to replace an ungrounded receptacle with a grounded one unless you can actually hook up the ground.

If you can't ground the outlet in the traditional manner, manufacturers have come up with a receptacle called a GFCI (ground fault circuit interrupter) that detects fluctuations in current and breaks the connection in a hurry. If the circuit trips, there is a reset button on the switch. Most codes now require GFCI outlets in kitchens and bathrooms. You can't fill a room with them, however, because they're so sensitive that they can start tripping each other.

Depending on where the outlet is in the "electrical run" you'll see different numbers of wires. The electrical run is defined by where it starts in the wall and where it ends. The "Beginning-of-the-Run" is the first outlet off the service wire into the run. The "End-of-the-Run" is the last one. Everything in between is called "Middle-of-the-Run." The "End-of-the-Run" and "Beginning-of-the-Run" receptacles will have only one *hot* wire and one *neutral*, whereas the "Middle-of-the-Run" receptacle will have two *hots*—one incoming and the other outgoing. The same with the *neutrals*.

Level: Beginner
Tools: Slotted screwdriver * Needle nose pliers * Circuit and continuity testers
Also: Electrical tape * Wire nuts (in some cases)

1) **SHUT OFF THE POWER, FRIENDS!**
Test to make sure. Take off the cover plate.

NOTE: Before you take things apart, spend a minute looking at how everything goes together. If you need to, draw a picture or make notes.

2) Remove the faulty receptacle by unscrewing the mounting screws. Loosen the terminal screws and remove the wires. All you have to do is take a good look at how they were put together and rewire them the same way. A double (or four receptacle outlet) is no more difficult than a single. It's just a few more wires to hook up and stuff back in the junction box.

3) The receptacle will have either screw terminals or push-in terminals. If you have push-ins, push the bare wire firmly into the hole. If you have screw terminals, proceed as follows.

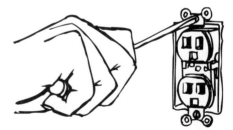

The wire in a junction box is solid as opposed to braided like Zip cord. It's bent into a hook and slid under the terminal screw. If you've got enough spare length of wire it's a good idea to snip off the old clip, expose fresh wire and make a new hook. Clean connections work best.

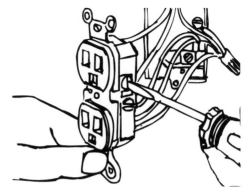

Slide the hook under the terminal screw so it's going in a clockwise direction; that way when you tighten the screw the hook will be drawn tightly into the terminal ensuring a solid connection.

The black wire goes to the brass screw and the white goes to the silver one. The green wire, if there is one, attaches to a little screw at the base of the receptacle.

4) When you're satisfied that all the connections are solid put everything back together the way you found it and test the circuit. Sometimes the most frustrating part of replacing an outlet is getting everything stuffed back in the box. Be patient—somebody got it in there, so believe it or not it all fits. The important thing is not to force the issue; you don't want to loosen connections or damage wires.

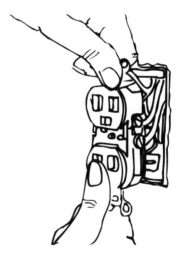

MAKE-IT-EASY PROJECT #7-6
Installing Switches

The process for changing a light switch is essentially the same as changing a receptacle. Remember how you took it apart, get the correctly rated replacement and go for it.

TURN THE POWER OFF BEFORE YOU BEGIN, AND USE YOUR CIRCUIT TESTER TO MAKE SURE.

Make-It-Easy Tip #31

SWITCHING SWITCHES—
THE OPPORTUNITIES ARE ENDLESS

Once you're a pro at replacing switches you can really start to customize the lighting system in your house. All you have to do is be sure that the switch you're adding to the system is rated correctly for where you're putting it. Get advice from your electrical connection at the hardware outlet and follow the detailed instructions that come with the specialty switches. You do have to make sure that your junction box is big enough to hold the replacement.

Here are some ideas:

• Add a DIMMER SWITCH to rooms in the house (like the dining room) where you would like to control the mood.

• A LOCKING SWITCH requires a key to open and ensures that an outlet controlling something important can't be turned on or off without your knowledge.

• A LIGHTED SWITCH can help you find it in the darkness of a basement or garage.

• A TIME-DELAY SWITCH allows you to get from one place to another before the light goes out.

• A TIMER SWITCH will turn the lights on and off at a specified time.

• A PILOT SWITCH has a light to remind you to turn out, say, a porch or backyard light before you go to bed.

• A MOTION DETECTOR SWITCH will sense movement and turn off a light as you leave a room.

There are four basic types of switches:

• Single Pole switches are still the most common. They simply open or close a single circuit when you toggle them up or down—on or off. "Poles" tell you the number of brass terminals available to connect "hot" wires.

• The Double Pole switch is an on/off switch with two *"hot"* connections and is used to control 240 volt outlets and major appliances.

• The Three Way switch gives you the ability to control a light from two different locations in a room or hallway.

• The Four Way switch controls an appliance, outlet or lighting fixture from three or more locations.

MAKE-IT-EASY PROJECT #7-7
Repairing and Replacing
Ceiling Fixtures

Just as trying to reach under the sink with a basin wrench to get to the mounting nuts on a faucet is the hardest part of faucet repair, the most difficult task in dealing with mounted lighting fixtures is getting to them. It figures, they're usually on the ceiling and that means a ladder. A lot of people are frightened of ladders and of heights; some get over it and some don't. One thing I know is that you should never get on a ladder unless you feel comfortable. It's not worth it.

If you do, however, working on a ceiling fixture is only slightly more difficult than working on a table lamp. The parts are essentially the same and so is the concept.

Level: Beginner to intermediate
Tools: Screwdriver * Needle nose pliers * Circuit tester
Also: Wire nuts (in some cases)

Shut down the power to the fixture at the service panel. Get your ladder in position, go up and have a look. This is where you'll appreciate having a tool belt to keep your hands free.

Ceiling lights are either the hanging type or mounted directly to the ceiling, like a globe fixture.

CHECK OUT LOW-VOLTAGE SYSTEMS— NOT JUST DOORBELLS

These days there are dozens of alternatives to the standard 120 volt systems. Low voltage systems come in all shapes and sizes and have some distinct advantages, including ease of installation and inexpensive operation. They're also safer to work on because of the tiny amount of electricity needed to operate them. You'll find low voltage systems supplying power to indirect lighting, track lighting, lights on staircases and pathways, and outdoor lighting. You can create dramatic effects on paintings and sculpture or even highlight the dining room table with light from a low voltage fixture, using, for example, pin spots with focusing panels and adjustable lenses. Low voltage strip lights are thin and narrow and can be mounted on bookshelves to add accent and focus.

Low voltage systems come in kits complete with the necessary transformer and hardware but you can put the components together yourself at the lighting store. It'll probably just be a little more expensive.

A low voltage system is definitely worth a look.

HANGING FIXTURES

1) If you're removing a hanging fixture you'll find a retaining screw somewhere on the cover plate. It may be either a slotted or Phillips screw. Remove the screw and lower the cover plate.

2) Once the plate is down you'll see the junction box, the mounting strap and the circuit wires. Remove the wire nuts carefully without touching the bare wires. Use the circuit tester to make sure the power is down and untwist the circuits.

3) Remove the retaining nut and lower the fixture to the floor for replacement or repair.

GLOBE FIXTURES

1) In most cases the globe is secured to the fixture base with retaining screws, but there are other ways of holding it in place such as tension clips. Remove the globe and the light bulbs.

2) You'll see two retaining screws in the fixture base. In some cases they need to be removed to lower the fixture; in others they just need to be loosened so the fixture can turn slightly and pull off.

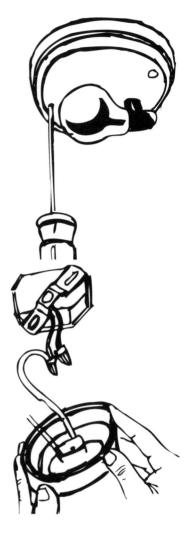

3) Pull the fixture away to reveal the junction box and wires. Twist off the wire nuts without touching bare wires and test for current again. If the power's off, untwist the wires and remove the fixture. Repair or replace according to manufacturer's instructions.

MAKE-IT-EASY PROJECT #7-8
Smoke Detectors—Yes!

Smoke detectors are so easy to install and so important to your family's safety that even if you do nothing else described in my book, I highly recommend you install them. If you've already got them please maintain them.

You should have smoke detectors on every floor of your home. They should be located between you and a potential source of fire such as the kitchen, attic or garage. Follow the manufacturer's instructions for placement.

Level: Beginner
Tools: Electric screwdriver * Stud finder * Tape measure (if necessary)

SHORT CIRCUITS, GROUND FAULTS AND OVERLOADS

A short circuit usually occurs when a cord frays or a plug is damaged. In either case the hot and the neutral wires come into contact and the circuit is "shortcutted" through that connection. This creates the flash you've probably seen when a plug or cord goes. Once the point of contact is burned away, the short is over, but you can see the black marks where it occurred and now you know exactly what to fix. Shorts can also occur if the connections to a switch or outlet are loose.

A ground fault, on the other hand, happens when a wire comes off a terminal inside a switch or junction box. The wire makes contact with the metal box and the current (seeking the path of least resistance) flows through the box back down to the main ground wire where most of it dissipates into the ground. In some cases not all the current will drain away so the box remains *"hot."* If you touch it you become the path of least resistance or the ground for that circuit. That's often what happens when people are accidentally electrocuted in their homes.

An overload happens when the circuit breaker or fuse is trying to carry more amperage than it can handle, commonly because too many fixtures or appliances are connected to the same circuit.

1) This doubles as a carpentry project, but since it's so easy I'll just go ahead and put it here. The base plate for the detector screws into the studs in your wall. You mount the plate, put in the battery and snap on the cover.

2) The smoke alarm kit comes with detailed mounting instructions and probably a paper template to give the exact placement of the screw holes. Follow the manufacturer's instructions for placement and use the stud finder to locate the nearest stud.

3) Use the template to mark the position of the holes. Use your center punch and a hammer to tap a little hole in the Sheetrock where you've made your marks. (This will give you a guide and make it easier to drive the screws.)

4) Screw in the base plate and assemble the detector.

ONCE THE SMOKE DETECTORS ARE IN PLACE DON'T FORGET TO MAINTAIN THEM. Set a regular schedule for battery replacement and stick to it. It could save your life. Ann Landers (of all people) says she changes the batteries once a year—on her birthday. That way she never forgets.

MAKE-IT-EASY PROJECT #7-9
Dealing with Shorts and Overloads

Two of the most common electrical problems in the home are shorts (either short circuits or ground faults) and overloads. Both will cause the breaker to flip and pitch you into darkness so it takes a little logic and common sense to figure out what the problem really is. Finding the source takes patience. But a pro has to be patient too and he's costing you money while he figures it out.

1) If a fuse or breaker is blowing constantly, the next time you replace it see how long before it goes again. If it blows in a hurry, it's likely that

you've got a case of the shorts. Usually that means a problem in a lamp, appliance, or its cord or in an extension cord. It's also possible it's in a ceiling fixture but that's less likely.

• Look for obvious damage like a frayed cord or a plug that's loose or very warm to the touch. If it's not the cords or connections, then the short's hidden deeper in the system.

2) There are a few things you can do before you call in an electrician.

• Unplug everything in the problem section, turn off all switches and get your continuity and circuit testers along with a slotted screwdriver.

• Turn off the breaker. If you use fuses, leave the blown fuse screwed loosely into the socket so no one will accidentally stick a finger in it. Don't forget the main power is still on.

• Check the outlets and switches for damage.

3) If the breaker or fuse takes a long time to blow, you've got an overload and the solution is to lighten the demand on the breaker. It's easy to figure out whether or not you've got enough watts available to do the job.

• Make a list of the wattage that appears on each light fixture and appliance in the area served by the circuit breaker that's blowing.

• Multiply the amperage of the circuit breaker by your service voltage. For example, let's say the circuit breaker is rated at 20 amps and your service is 120 volts: 20 X 120 volts = 2400 watts of potential use. If you have more watts on your list than the circuit breaker can handle, unplug enough appliances or fixtures so you are under the limit or upgrade the service and breaker to suit your needs.

SWITCHES. To make sure the current is really down, turn the switches on and off. Remove the cover plate, take the circuit tester and touch one of the probes to a terminal screw and one to the junction box. Do the same with the other screw. The light should stay off. Use the continuity tester to check for a fault in the switch itself. If you find a faulty switch, replace it, and you've probably solved the problem.

OUTLETS. Insert the tips of the circuit tester in the slots of the outlet. If the little light at the top doesn't go on, it's safe to remove the cover plate and begin working.

• Take a small slotted screwdriver, remove the screws that hold the switch or receptacle in place and gently pull the unit out of its junction box. Look for obvious damage, like broken receptacles or loose wires. Take your continuity tester and clip the little alligator clip to one of the terminal screws; touch the tip of the tester probe to the other screw. If the little light goes on, the switch is good. Put it back together and back in the box.

NOTE: With both switches and outlets check the screws that hold the terminal wires in place to see if any have loosened; if so, tighten them down. Vibration can cause screws to loosen. If you find something obvious like a terminal wire that's come totally off the switch or receptacle, screw it back into place. Sometimes it's that simple.

• After you've checked all the receptacles and switches put them back in their boxes. Turn the switches to the off position. (You can leave the cover plates off just in case you have to go back in.)

• Turn on the power. Flip the switches one by one and see what happens. Plug something into the outlets. If a wall switch controls an outlet, plug something into the outlet. If the circuit blows, the problem may be inside the fixture or appliance controlled by the switch or outlet.

If, after all this, the problem won't go away, you've got to call in the pros, but at least you know that you've done everything possible to protect your checking account and you've got information they can use to speed up the repair.

A FINAL NOTE

If you get ambitious later on down the line and decide to rewire the basement you'll need to get a permit. Why? Safety codes and installation guidelines are the result of extensive testing and field experience. While it might be a pain in the neck to deal with the inspectors, it's nowhere near as bad as getting something done and finding out too late it was wrong. Improperly installed wiring can also be dangerous if not fixed, and replacing it will most certainly make an unexpected and major dent in your checking account.

CHAPTER EIGHT

Heating, Cooling, Insulation & Weatherproofing

The heating and cooling systems in your home are a classic combination of the simple and complex. Certain repairs and maintenance are best left to the professionals but still there are several things you can do on a regular basis, like replacing filters and lubricating motors, to help your systems run smoothly.

Heating and cooling maintenance also goes hand in hand with efficient insulation and weatherproofing. No matter how much your systems cost they won't work effectively in a leaky house. In the old days there wasn't much you could do about drafts. But that's no longer true. All it takes today is a trip to the hardware store to see the vast array of kits available that make sealing leaks an easy weekend project. When you realize how much money you will save on heating and cooling

TOOLS OF THE TRADE—Heating and Cooling

• Tools You'll Use from Your Basic Kit

Adjustable Wrench	Gloves	Slotted
Clean Rags	Mat Knife	Screwdrivers
Drip Pan or Small	Phillips	Socket Wrench
Bucket	Screwdrivers	Staple Gun
Flashlight		Toothbrush

bills in the long run, you will quickly see that it's worth your while to do a little weatherproofing and insulating. A well-sealed and insulated home adds considerably to your quality of life and will provide a new level of comfort.

MORE TOOLS OF THE TRADE

Here are some specialty tools you'll want to consider adding to your collection as you go along.

BOTTLE BRUSH Stiff bristled and used for cleaning the insides of bottles, it also works well to remove dirt from furnace blower blades.

OIL CAN An oil can with a long narrow nozzle is a must for lubricating furnace motors and bearings.

SOFT BRUSH A soft brush is useful for cleaning dirt and debris from surfaces and air conditioner coils.

FIN COMB A special tool used to straighten the fins in an air conditioner.

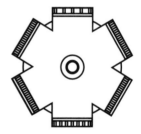

CAULKING GUN A pistol-like device that holds cartridges of caulk, making them easier to apply.

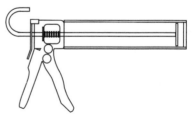

ALSO: A vacuum cleaner and attachments.

INSULATION AND WEATHERPROOFING— SEALING UP THE HOUSE

MAKE-IT-EASY PROJECT #8-1
Several Ways to Make Your Home More Energy Efficient

Level: Beginner
Tools: Caulking gun
Materials: Silicone caulk (sold in tubes) * Expandable insulating foam (comes in an aerosol can) * Fiberglass insulation

After arming yourself with your caulking gun and expandable foam, go outside and take a walk around your house. Look for vents and other things that are attached to the sides.

1) Use the caulk to seal around vents, plumbing lines, at joints where unlike materials meet (like a cement porch or foundation and wooden siding), windows, doors, and electrical fixtures.

NOTE: Remember to smooth the caulk into the seam with a wet finger.

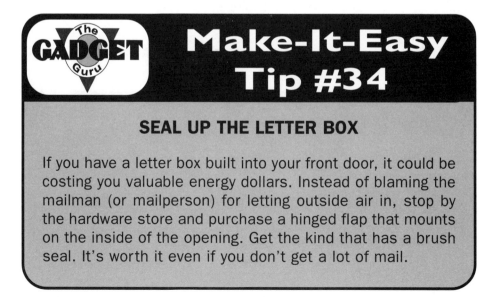

Make-It-Easy Tip #34

SEAL UP THE LETTER BOX

If you have a letter box built into your front door, it could be costing you valuable energy dollars. Instead of blaming the mailman (or mailperson) for letting outside air in, stop by the hardware store and purchase a hinged flap that mounts on the inside of the opening. Get the kind that has a brush seal. It's worth it even if you don't get a lot of mail.

2) Use the expandable foam to seal large gaps around water spigots, cable and telephone hookups. You should wear gloves when you work with expandable foam.

3) Use pieces of fiberglass insulation to seal the joists at the top of the foundation in the basement. Fill the openings loosely but not so loosely the stuff will fall out.

MAKE-IT-EASY PROJECT #8-2
Insulating and Sealing Windows

Level: Beginner
Tools: Candle * Staple gun * Small hammer * Hair dryer
Also: Various kinds of weather stripping as necessary, including:
          Good quality hollow neoprene strips * Tension strips * Plastic
          shrink wrap window coverings

A lot of money flows out of your house through drafty windows. The Department of Energy says the loss can be as much as 35 percent. The

Make-It-Easy
Tip #35

DON'T PACK IT IN—AN INSULATION TIP

Insulation should never be compressed; the more tightly it's packed, the less effective it is.

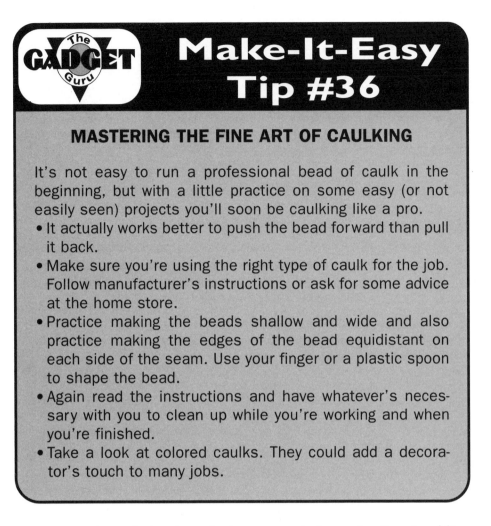

Make-It-Easy Tip #36

MASTERING THE FINE ART OF CAULKING

It's not easy to run a professional bead of caulk in the beginning, but with a little practice on some easy (or not easily seen) projects you'll soon be caulking like a pro.

- It actually works better to push the bead forward than pull it back.
- Make sure you're using the right type of caulk for the job. Follow manufacturer's instructions or ask for some advice at the home store.
- Practice making the beads shallow and wide and also practice making the edges of the bead equidistant on each side of the seam. Use your finger or a plastic spoon to shape the bead.
- Again read the instructions and have whatever's necessary with you to clean up while you're working and when you're finished.
- Take a look at colored caulks. They could add a decorator's touch to many jobs.

most expensive solution is replacing your windows. Another is adding storm windows, but they're also an expensive installation. There are other solutions that are a little easier on your pocketbook until you're ready to take the economic plunge. Most weather-stripping systems come complete with the right hardware.

1) The most efficient way to test for air leaks in your windows is to check each one with a lighted candle on a windy day. Move the candle around the edges of the window and see if it flickers. If it does (and I'll bet you dollars to donuts it does) you've got some projects to tackle.

2) If the leaks are at the top and bottom of the sash (the frame that holds the glass), staple good quality hollow self-adhesive neoprene strips to the outside edges according to manufacturer's instructions.

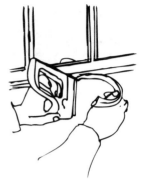

3) If the leak is between the top and bottom sashes nail a tension strip to the inside face of the bottom rail of the top sash. You'll have to raise the bottom window and lower the top until you can get to it. Again follow the manufacturer's instructions. (It's easier than it sounds.)

4) Seal the entire outside edge of the window with acrylic latex silicone caulk. Don't use clear because you can't paint over it.

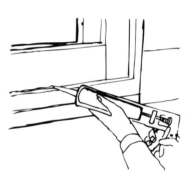

5) If the leaks are around the tracks where the windows move up and down you can talk to your home supply expert about installing metal "v-channels." A quicker fix if you're not planning to open the window until spring is to use *peelable* caulk (you can pull it off when you want to without damaging the surfaces) to seal around the inside edges of the window.

WRAP UP THOSE DUCTS AND PIPES

A lot of plumbing and duct work runs through unheated parts of your house, like unfinished basements and crawl-spaces. Heating supply stores sell the right kinds of insulation for air conditioning and heating ducts as well as foam tubing and insulating tape for exposed pipes. They're easy to install and every insulation project you do adds up to savings. A little bit here and a little bit there will pay big dividends in the long run.

6) If all else fails use plastic "shrink wrap" to cover the entire window. You install the wrap according to instructions and use a hair dryer to remove wrinkles. Usually a double faced tape is run on the outside edge of the window, the shrink wrap is applied and trimmed and then wrinkles are removed with the hair dryer. The plastic can be removed at winter's end. The best quality products are almost invisible if installed correctly.

NOTE: There are many kinds of weather stripping systems for outside or entrance doors. They work on the same principles as those for windows and they're well worth checking out.

MAKE-IT-EASY PROJECT #8-3
Installing Insulation in an Unfinished Attic

Putting insulation in the attic is a project well within the range of the beginning to intermediate do-it-yourselfer. Not only that—it's smart. Make a good plan and follow it carefully. By doing it yourself you're saving a huge percentage of what it would cost you to have someone else do it.

When you're working in an unfinished attic you'll need a sheet of plywood to spread across the floor joists so you'll have a safe and secure work space. Move carefully across floor joists and don't step between them; you might put a foot through the ceiling below.

Level: Beginner to intermediate
Tools: Tape measure * Mat knife * Hand or electric stapler *
           Hammer

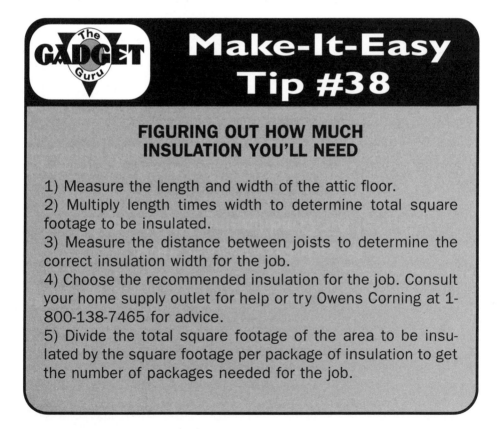

Make-It-Easy
Tip #38

FIGURING OUT HOW MUCH
INSULATION YOU'LL NEED

1) Measure the length and width of the attic floor.
2) Multiply length times width to determine total square footage to be insulated.
3) Measure the distance between joists to determine the correct insulation width for the job.
4) Choose the recommended insulation for the job. Consult your home supply outlet for help or try Owens Corning at 1-800-138-7465 for advice.
5) Divide the total square footage of the area to be insulated by the square footage per package of insulation to get the number of packages needed for the job.

HANDLING AND CUTTING INSULATION

It's a good idea to leave the insulation in its wrapper until you're ready to use it. The stuff expands a lot after it's opened. Keep your gloves, respirator and glasses on at all times. Fiberglass is safe to work with as long as you take simple steps to protect yourself. This stuff can itch.

When you're cutting the insulation, lay it on your temporary floor face down. Use the straight board to mark where you want to cut and press firmly with the mat knife using the board as a guide.

Also: Straight board (for cutting insulation) * Worklight * Sheet of plywood (working and cutting surface) * Broom handle or rake (to shove insulation into corners)

Protective
Equipment: Work gloves * Loose-fitting long sleeved shirt * OSHA approved safety glasses * 3M 8710 disposable dust respirator

Materials: Insulation* Baffles (ventilation troughs—see Step 1 below for description)

1) Lay temporary flooring (your plywood sheet) and hang a worklight so you can see what you're doing. Before you begin to lay down the insulation install the baffles. **BAFFLES** are plastic troughs that are stapled between the rafters with a staple gun. They keep the insulation from covering eaves vents and make sure they can do their job, which is keeping fresh air circulating in the attic.

2) Once the baffles are stapled up put on your safety glasses and respirator. Begin laying insulation faced side down at the outer edge of your attic and work toward the center.

3) Lay in long runs first and use leftovers for shorter spaces. Ends of insulation should be cut to fit snugly around crossbracing. The insula-

tion should extend far enough to cover exterior walls without blocking the eaves vents. Staple as necessary to hold insulation in corners but the less the better.

4) If you have recessed lighting fixtures, the insulation must be kept at least 3 inches from the fixture. You do this by installing dams, which are simply pieces of wood inserted between the joists to keep the insulation at bay.

Make-It-Easy Project #8-4
Balancing a Forced Air Heating System

Adjusting the air flowing through a forced air heating system is called balancing. It's done to make sure that each room receives an equal amount of heat through the registers. Like tracing a short circuit, it requires a little detective work and a few trips around the house. Balance the system during cold weather to get the best results.

1) With the furnace running at its optimum level, walk through the house and note the rooms that are too warm and those that are too cold. While the registers in each room have adjustable louvers, their purpose is more to direct air flow than to bring more volume into the room. The next step is to find the dampers.

2) Since the **DAMPERS** are spaced throughout the ducting system, you'll have to seek them out, but they usually aren't too hard to find. They'll probably be in the basement. Like the damper on a fireplace they control the flow of warm air by the degree to which the metal plate inside is open or closed. Again, like the damper in a fireplace, they are controlled by a handle on the outside of the duct.

3) Make adjustments in the hottest room first, adjusting the damper until the room is comfortable. Reducing the flow of air in the hottest room moves more warm air to other rooms. Once you've made the hottest room comfortable, move to the next hottest and so on until you've set a basic damper position for each room in the house. Remember it takes a

while for each room to warm up after you've adjusted a damper so be patient. This process can take several days but it's worth it.

4) When all the rooms are pretty comfortable you can make more subtle adjustments on the dampers until everything is how you want it. Once every room is set, mark the damper positions with some paint or a permanent marker so you don't have to do it again later.

NOTE: If you still have cold rooms after balancing the system you may need to call in a professional to adjust the speed of the main blower (sometimes called a *squirrel-cage*) in the furnace to force more air into the system. He'll either adjust or replace the drive pulleys on the fan motor.

MAKE-IT-EASY PROJECT #8-5
Replacing or Servicing Furnace Filters

Cleaning and servicing the filters on your heating and cooling systems are sure ways to make them operate more effectively and economically. It's easy to do and, as I said earlier, something that I learned about through an expensive experience when I had to call in a company to clean all the ducting in my house. Preventive maintenance saves money, time and aggravation.

Your manual will suggest how often filters should be cleaned or replaced. It can be as often as once a month if the system is given heavy use. But you should check them regularly in any case.

There are several different styles and kinds of furnace filters depending on the make and model of the unit. Check the booklet that came with yours to see what you need and how to do it. Most filters, however, are dealt with as follows.

REPLACING A DISPOSABLE FILTER ELEMENT OR CLEANING A PERMANENT ONE

Level: Beginner
Materials: Replacement filter (if needed)

In some furnaces the filter element lives in a slot between the return duct and the blower. You can get to it without having to shut off the furnace because the filter simply slides in and out of its slot for replacement or cleaning. In others, it's inside the furnace and you'll have to shut the power down and pull off the front panels to get to it.

Some filters are simply removed and replaced when they get dirty; others can be flushed clean with a garden hose and reinserted.

If you're replacing make sure to use an exact duplicate. Have several on hand. You can buy them in bulk. This is a regular maintenance chore.

NOTE: Make sure you have the filter placed in the correct way. There will be an arrow on the side of the filter that displays the air flow.

1) Remove the filter and hold it up to a strong light. If you can see through it easily you're fine, but if it's blocked replace or clean it if you can.

SERVICING AN ELECTRONIC FILTER

You should clean an electronic filter at least once a month.

Level: Beginner
Materials: Replacement filter (if needed)

1) Shut down the furnace and open the filter door.

2) Slide out the electronic filter and look at it for damage. If there are problems replace it. Otherwise, wash the filter carefully in a solution of detergent and water. Rinse it well and allow to dry thoroughly before putting it back.

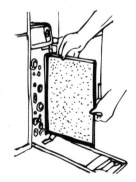

3) The electronic cells should be cleaned once a year. Follow the instructions in the manual for removing and cleaning them.

SERVICING A HAMMOCK STYLE FILTER

You should inspect a hammock for dirt and debris at least once a month when the furnace is getting heavy use.

Level: Beginner
Tools: Mat knife * Gloves * Flashlight
Materials: Fiberglass batting (comes in rolls from a heating supply dealer)

1) Turn off the furnace and its breaker at the panel. Remove the panels that cover the furnace and set them aside. Take a look at the filter by shining the flashlight through it from the back. If it's dirty do the following:

2) Put on your gloves and release the wire hammock from its rails. Fold the hammock down and pull it out.

3) Remove the old filter and cut a new piece of batting to size with the mat knife. Replace the filter and slide the hammock back into place.

4) If you have a direct drive blower you might as well clean the blades while you are inside the furnace. Use a toothbrush to clean each blade. If you can fit a vacuum cleaner attachment inside, use that as well. If it's too tough to reach, the unit will have to be removed and you might consider calling in a professional.

5) Restore the panels and turn on the furnace.

6) Put the old filter into a plastic bag and seal it before throwing it out.

NOTE: Be sure to find out if fiberglass requires special disposal in your area before dumping your old filter in the garbage.

MAKE-IT-EASY PROJECT #8-6
Cleaning Furnace Blower Blades That Are Belt Driven

If you maintain the filters on a regular basis the blower blades will stay pretty clean. If you don't, eventually you'll have to clean them because dirty blades not only are inefficient, but blow dirt and debris into your home.

Level: Beginner
Tools: Socket wrench * Vacuum cleaner
Also: Someone to help you slide the blower out of the furnace

1) Shut off the furnace and main breaker. Remove the service panels to expose the blower.

2) Use a socket wrench to remove the bolts that hold the blower to its mounting rails.

3) With the help of your assistant slide the blower assembly out of the furnace. Use the brush attachment on your vacuum to clean the blade. Bang the side of the case to loosen dirt and clean the side as well.

4) Slide the unit back into the furnace and rebolt it to the mounting rails. Now you understand
why it's a good idea to maintain
the filters on a regular basis.

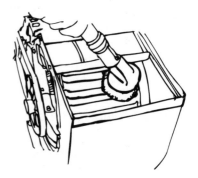

MAKE-IT-EASY PROJECT #8-7
Lubricating the Blower Motor

This should be done once a year.

Level: Beginner
Tools: Oil can with non-detergent SAE-30 motor oil * Screwdriver

1) Shut down the furnace and the breaker. Remove the service panel to the motor. You will probably find instructions for lubricating and maintenance on the inside of the panel.

2) Find the lubrication cups and squirt a few drops into them. Follow the instructions on the panel—don't over-oil. The openings may be covered by some sort of cap. If so you'll need a screwdriver to pry off the cap. Replace it after oiling.

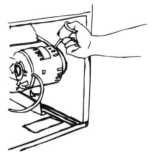

MAKE-IT-EASY PROJECT #8-8
Maintaining an Oil Burner

To keep you warm and cozy without costing you a fortune, your furnace, whether gas or oil, needs yearly maintenance from a professional. Unless you're really gung-ho and very skilled the combustion systems are too complex to be worth mastering by the average do-it-yourselfer.

But there are routine maintenance tasks that don't involve adjustments to the sensitive components that fire your furnace. Do the following at the beginning of the heating season. If the furnace is getting a lot of use it's a good idea to repeat the process around mid-winter.

Level: Beginner to intermediate
Tools: Adjustable wrench * Drip pan or small bucket * Toothbrush
          * Clean rags * Bottle brush * Oil can

Materials: Replacement oil filter * Replacement filter gasket * Cleaning solvent (for soaking pump strainer if your burner has one) * Non-detergent electric motor oil (SAE-10 or SAE-30)

1) Shut off the furnace main switch and the furnace breaker at your main panel. Also shut off the oil supply valve.

2) Place the drip pan or bucket under the oil filter and remove it from the housing. Some models screw in and some are held by a bolt that sits on top of the filter.

3) Drain excess oil into the bucket and dump the filter into the bucket or pan. Wipe out the filter cup with a clean rag and insert new filter and gasket. Screw or bolt the filter cup firmly back on the housing lid. Turn on the oil supply valve. Check with local authorities for how to dispose of the old oil.

4) If the motor on your oil burner is not self-lubricating you'll see what are called oil cups, or **PORTS**, on each end of the motor. Use your oil can and lubricate with a few drops of non-detergent electric motor oil. See the manual for the recommended weight. It's usually SAE-10 or 30.

5) If your burner has a pump strainer, you'll find it on one end of the unit. Use your adjustable wrench to remove the cover nuts and remove the cover. Pull off the strainer and the gasket. Check the strainer for damage. If it's OK, soak the strainer in cleaning solvent. Clean it thoroughly with the toothbrush. Put on a new gasket and replace the strainer, then put the cover back on.

6) To clean the fan, unbolt the transformer on top of the burner (it usually swings aside) and clean the blades with a bottle brush, toothbrush or clean rags. Also use a clean rag to wipe down the interior of the fan housing. Swing the transformer back into place and tighten it down.

MAKE-IT-EASY PROJECT #8-9
Central Air Conditioning Maintenance

Cleaning the coils and fins in your evaporator and condenser at the beginning of each summer will go a long way to extending their life and will cut down on costly repairs to this most important system in your home.

Level: Beginner
Tools: Soft brush * Fin comb * Slotted screwdriver * Level * Oil can
Also: Garden hose and gloves

MAINTAINING THE EVAPORATOR

In some systems the evaporator is sealed and only a technician can work on it. Sometimes you can have an access panel installed to get you in so you can do cleaning maintenance yourself. But in many systems the panel is already in place.

1) Turn off the air conditioner and furnace. Also shut off the main breaker and the outdoor disconnect. Remove the panel and set it aside.

2) Put on your gloves because there are sharp edges all over the place in an evaporating unit. Use the soft brush to gently clean away dirt from the coils and fins.

3) Examine the fins and see if any are bent. Gently straighten them by inserting the fin comb and pulling it through.

4) Wipe as much sediment and algae as possible from the drain pan and then flush it out with a hose. Since algae love drain pans, you can add a half cup of bleach to the water in the pan or use a special pill according to instructions in the manual to control them.

5) Replace the panel and switch everything back on.

MAINTAINING THE CONDENSER UNIT

Level: Beginner
Tools: Soft brush * Fin comb * Slotted screwdriver * Level * Oil can
Also: Garden hose and gloves

LUBRICATING THE FAN MOTOR

1) Shut off all disconnects and the main breaker to the system.

2) Check the condenser with your level. It must be sitting square. If the slab that the unit sits on has shifted during the winter, the condenser won't work properly and you'll have to have someone come in and level it.

3) Take off the fan grill by removing the screws. Remove the blades and oil the fan motor through the ports or cups.

4) Check the coils for dirt and debris and also look for bent fins. Clean the coils with a soft brush and use the fin comb to straighten bent fins. Clear out any leaves, sticks or other debris that may have settled inside the unit.

5) Flush the coils with the hose, first from the inside and then from the outside to loosen and remove dirt.

6) Replace the blades and the grill.

MAKE-IT-EASY PROJECT #8-10
Maintaining a Window Mounted Air Conditioner

Many of the working parts of modern window air conditioners are permanently lubricated and factory sealed. But there are several maintenance tasks you can perform to keep your window unit working efficiently. It's a good idea to have the unit serviced once a year to make sure the refrigerant is up to snuff.

One of the most important tasks is cleaning the filter at least once a month. Another is frequent vacuuming of the condenser coil. If you leave the unit in the window during the winter, purchase a cover and use it. You'll add years to the air conditioner's life.

Level: Beginner
Tools: Fin comb * Screwdriver * Putty knife
Materials: Replacement filter (if necessary)
Also: Rags * Non-detergent motor oil * Vacuum cleaner and
            attachments

1) Unplug the air conditioner. Remove the grill. It will be held in place by either plastic tabs or spring clips. (Check the manual.)

2) Remove the filter. If it's a disposable type, replace it. If it can be cleaned and reused, wash it thoroughly in warm soapy water. Let it dry thoroughly before putting it back.

3) While the filter is off, check the fins in the condenser coil and use the fin comb to straighten any that are bent. (See Make-It-Easy Project #8-9.) Vacuum the fins with a soft brush attachment. If the evaporator fins are extremely clogged, flush with water to loosen debris.

Make-It-Easy Tip #40

The GADGET Guru

AN ENERGY EFFICIENT YEAR ROUND CHECK LIST FOR YOUR HOME

My friends at Owens Corning (who know something about insulation) have come up with some tips to conserve energy and save money.

• According to the Department of Energy, draft proofing your home can cut your electric bill by 10 percent. On a windy day, hold a candle next to windows, doors, electrical boxes, outlets, switches, plumbing fixtures, keyholes, letterbox flaps and other places where there is a possible air path to the outside. If the candle flickers you know you've got a leak and need to seal it.
• Caulk, weather strip and otherwise seal against drafts: windows and door frames, plumbing fixtures, electrical outlets and switches. (Insulating foam gaskets cut to fit inside the receptacle come packaged in quantity; to install one all you have to do is remove the cover plate and fit the foam gasket in place.) Take a look outside as well and seal around windows and doors.
• Close off unoccupied rooms.
• Insulate your hot water heater, pipes and ducts.
• Install water-saver shower heads or flow restrictors. They will pay for themselves in months.
• Consider installing energy efficient doors and windows, which can help reduce fuel costs up to 15 percent.
• Choose energy efficient kitchen appliances. They might cost a bit more but will save you money in the long run.

CHAPTER NINE

Strapping on the Tool Belt— **Carpentry and Woodworking**

I think that carpentry and woodworking projects are some of the most exciting you'll take on as a household guru. The reason is simple. You get to see the fruits of your labor when you're done and you can show your successes to family and friends. It's all very satisfying in my humble opinion. Making or fixing something you see and touch every day is a very positive experience.

When you start getting into the carpentry end of home repair your tool collection is going to begin to grow and you'll soon discover why you

Make-It-Easy Tip #41

A POCKETFUL OF TAPE MEASURES

I don't know what the dollar is actually worth today. I'm sure it's shrinking in value but it's still exactly six inches long. Inflation aside, it can still work as a measuring tool in a crunch.

TOOLS OF THE TRADE—
Carpentry and Woodworking

• Tools You'll Use from Your Basic Kit

Adjustable Wrench	Electric Screwdriver	Pliers
Carpenter's Awl	Electrician's Tape	Pry Bar
Carpenter's Level	Extension Cords	Putty Knife
Carpenter's Pencils	Flashlight	Screwdrivers
Chalk Line	Florist's Wire	Socket Wrench
Channel Lock Pliers	Framing Square	Staple Gun
Clamps	Glue Gun	Tape Measure
Handsaw	Hammer	Three Prong Grounding Adapter
Combination Square	Masking Tape	Tool Belt
Electric Drill	Mat Knife	Torpedo Level
	Nail Set	Twine
	Needle Nose Pliers	Work Gloves

need to set aside an area of the house that will become your workshop. There has to be a place to put things because pretty soon your tool box will be bulging. You'll also need a place to work on things that you don't want to do *on site* as the professionals say. But building the arsenal that helps you keep your house in order is part of the fun of home repair.

We're going to spend a little more time here talking about tools, tool safety and materials because a little basic information is helpful when you're trying to figure out what kind of projects you feel ready to try on for size.

TUNE IN AND GO BEYOND THE BASICS—
IT'S NOT JUST THIS OLD HOUSE *ANYMORE*

Take a little cruise around the cable with your remote and you'll see that TV networks and producers are into do-it-yourself in a big way. A home improvement show seems to be playing somewhere 24 hours a day. And once you've started to get a grasp of the basics of home repair and maintenance these shows can really help you hone your skills and give you confidence to attempt tougher projects. Also check them out for short-cuts, tips and new project ideas.

MORE TOOLS OF THE TRADE

Here are some woodworking and carpentry tools you'll want to consider adding to your collection as you need them.

BELT SANDER Belt sanders make fast work of sanding all kinds of surfaces. Shop around for one that's user friendly. Just like regular sandpaper the belts come in many different grades of grit.

BEVEL GAUGE These handy and inexpensive items have an adjustable blade that allows you to mark or copy an angle.

CHISELS Wood chisels are used to do fine cutting and shaping and require practice to use properly, but as your skills grow you'll be adding them to your tool box.

CIRCULAR SAW Circular saws make cutting lumber and plywood easy and produce accurate results. For most home repair, I recommend the models with 4½ inch blades. They're light and easy to handle. Manufacturers like Black and Decker and Skil are coming out

WOOD PUTTY—*THE CARPENTER'S FRIEND*

Wood putty is a compound used to fill holes left from counter-sinking (setting below the surface) nails and screws. These days it comes in colors to match stains and finishes and is essential for repairing and finishing your woodworking projects. Use a putty knife to force the compound into the hole (fill the hole to a point slightly above the surface; that way you can sand it down to flush after it's dried).

with battery operated models that are well worth checking out.

Circular saws cut upwards, meaning the blade is cutting from the bottom of the wood to the top. That means that the cleanest or "finish" cut will be on the bottom of the material. You need to decide which side of the work is going to be the top and measure and mark cut lines accordingly.

While there are many options for blades you should start with a combination type that cuts with and against the wood grain. The right blade can cut metal too. Practice using the tool on scrap lumber until you are comfortable with it and follow all the safety procedures. (See the safety tips on p. 157.)

COMPASS Compasses are used for transferring very accurate measurements from one surface to another, and, of course, they draw circles.

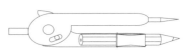

DUST MASKS AND RESPI-RATORS Sometimes materials and products we need to use to fix things around the house aren't good for us to breathe while we're applying them. Follow the manufacturer's instructions carefully and use what is recommended as protection.

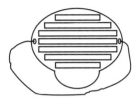

FILES Files are truly multipurpose tools; they get into tight places and take off rough edges. They've been around for thousands of years so you might as well have a few in your tool box. There are many shapes and sizes. Consider four different types—full, round, half round, and flat. You can also get removable wooden handles to make using them easier.

JIGSAW I think everybody should have a jigsaw. They are versatile and easy to use, and simply by changing the blade you can cut wood, metal and plastic. Get one with variable speeds. I recommend learning to use a jigsaw before you tackle a circular saw.

MALLET Mallets are hammers faced with cowhide, rubber or plastic. They're used anytime something needs to be hit (like a chisel) or adjusted (like a shelf) without damaging the surface.

MITER BOX Miter boxes are used with special fine tooth saws to cut accurate angles in molding and trim. If you decide to make picture frames, for instance, a miter box is an essential investment.

NAIL APRON Nail aprons hold pencils and nails and they're lighter than tool belts, but they also help with safety. They keep loose clothing from dangling over your work. Home supply outlets often give them away for free; all you have to do is wear their advertising.

ORBITAL SANDERS Orbital sanders are used for fine finish sanding. Unlike a belt sander, the sandpaper moves in a circular motion and won't scratch or mar the work. I recommend having one around.

SAFETY GLASSES Common sense eye protection. Enough said.

TIN SNIPS Essentially scissors with strong blades for cutting metal.

WOOD PLANES Planes are also ancient woodworking tools. There are many different shapes and sizes. They smooth and shape wood.

WORKMATE Black and Decker came up with an amazing invention. I don't know how I got along before I got mine. A truly portable workbench and well worth the investment.

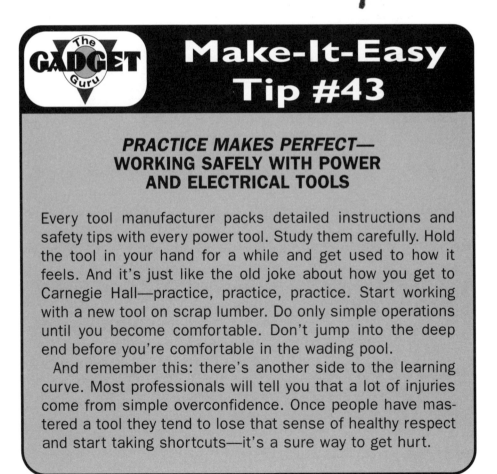

G**ADG**ET The Guru

Make-It-Easy Tip #43

PRACTICE MAKES PERFECT—
WORKING SAFELY WITH POWER
AND ELECTRICAL TOOLS

Every tool manufacturer packs detailed instructions and safety tips with every power tool. Study them carefully. Hold the tool in your hand for a while and get used to how it feels. And it's just like the old joke about how you get to Carnegie Hall—practice, practice, practice. Start working with a new tool on scrap lumber. Do only simple operations until you become comfortable. Don't jump into the deep end before you're comfortable in the wading pool.

And remember this: there's another side to the learning curve. Most professionals will tell you that a lot of injuries come from simple overconfidence. Once people have mastered a tool they tend to lose that sense of healthy respect and start taking shortcuts—it's a sure way to get hurt.

The GADGET Guru Make-It-Easy Tip #44

CLAMPS—*YOUR SILENT ASSISTANT*

Having the right set of clamps around when you're doing a job is like having a helper you don't have to pay (except once). Not only are they an extra hand and a safety factor when you're cutting materials but they guarantee that a joint you're regluing will be tight and strong. I keep several different kinds around the house.

• **C-clamps** are "c" shaped with an adjustable screw on one end. They're great for holding materials securely on a work surface. C-clamps are inexpensive and come in many different sizes. They should be your first clamp purchase.

• **Spring clamps** have plastic tips to protect the materials. These clips are very strong and versatile. They come in a variety of sizes.

• **Miter clamps** are used to hold 45 degree angles together for nailing and gluing. Perfect for assembling picture frames.

Better Safe than Sorry—
SAFETY TIPS FROM THE PROS

Professionals take good care of their tools but they also take good care of themselves. Sure it's an issue of safety, but it's a practical matter as well. Taking time off because of an injury takes money out of their pockets. Good crafts-people have a healthy respect for the good things their tools can do and for the bad things as well. They have to—it's how they make their living.

While you and I don't make our livings with hammers and saws, the same principles of healthy respect and safety apply to us as well. It doesn't matter how beautifully a project turns out if we hurt ourselves while we're doing it.

When I started working with power tools I had already mastered the art of hammering a nail and cutting a board with a handsaw. In fact I was pretty good at it and I recommend you practice these skills, too.

But when it came to power tools, I remember being a little scared. Well, actually terrified, and why not? They're noisy, maybe a little heavy and awkward in the beginning, and they might seem more like weapons than tools. But I was really interested in doing projects that required their use and so I decided to go for it. I took a very cautious approach. I read the manuals carefully, paying particular attention to the safety tips. I started on the simplest level possible and didn't try anything I wasn't positive I could handle. I went to my friends at the hardware store and got firsthand demonstrations and up-close and personal tips. I even took a couple of workshops.

What I learned was that respecting what's potentially dangerous about power tools made me pay close attention to what I was doing and be very careful. Respect is like positive fear, it keeps you alert. And if you stick with it you can learn to use any power tool made with confidence and safety.

SOME SAFETY BASICS

POWER TOOL SAFETY

• Always wear eye protection and don't wear loose clothing or dangling jewelry. You don't want to get tangled up in the tool.

• Before you use any power tool check it carefully to make sure it's in good condition. For instance, are the blades sharp and tight? Are the cord and plug in good shape? Does it sound right when you turn it on?

• Always unplug a power tool before changing the blade or making any adjustments.

• Know where your extension cord is at all times. Drape it over your shoulder or hold it in your free hand so there's no danger of cutting it by accident.

• Don't force a tool to do a job. You can tell when it's running smoothly, trust it. Slow and steady wins the race. If you are cutting large boards, always clamp them to the work surface.

• If a tool jams or freezes, shut it off and see what the problem is before you try it again.

• Don't defeat any of the safety mechanisms, no matter what a pain in the neck they might seem to be. A lot of research went into putting them there and they exist for a reason.

• Never set a circular saw down until the blade's stopped turning.

• If a tool breaks or a cord goes bad, repair it immediately or mark it with tape so you'll remember to repair it. Pros sometimes clip the plug off a bad cord so the tool can't be used until it's fixed.

WORK AREA SAFETY

• Keep your work area clear of debris and free of sawdust. You don't want to stumble over something or slip while you're using a tool.

• Make sure the circuit breakers and your extension cord are rated to handle the tools you're using. Don't ever use Zip cord, ever!

• Have a smoke detector in your work area.

• Keep a dry chemical fire extinguisher (ABC rating) in the work area because it'll deal with combustible and electrical fires.

• Consider installing locking switches to keep the outlets around the work area dead when you're not using them. If possible keep power tools locked away and hide the key.

• Make sure you've got plenty of good light to see with. Add work lights if necessary so there aren't any shadows on your project.

THE GADGET GURU'S FYI—
A BASIC GUIDE TO MATERIALS AND HARDWARE

WOOD—THE BASICS

There are hundreds of species of wood, but for the carpenter there are two basic classifications—hard and soft. Hard wood comes from trees with leaves (like oak) and soft wood comes from trees with cones (like fir or pine). Hard woods really are hard, as in dense; they're also hard to work with. Unless you become the next finish carpenter on *This Old House*, you'll be working with soft woods.

LUMBERYARD JARGON REVEALED

DIMENSIONS

Lumber is measured by its thickness and its width and then its length. The first dimension is always the thickness, the second is always the width and the third is always the length. So, it would logically follow that a 1 X 3 X 12 would be one inch thick by three inches wide by 12 feet long. Sorry friends, but it isn't the case. The first two dimensions (length and width) are called **NOMINAL DIMENSIONS** and are actually the size of the board before it's milled and finished at the sawmill. For instance, standard 1 X 3 actually measures approximately ¾ inch by 2¾ inches. It will, however, be 12 feet long. This is a piece of information you really need when you're doing a project where the measurements need to be exact.

GRADES

What you're using the wood for is your guide for the quality you need to buy. Lumber is graded by quality from A to D. Top quality lumber (also called **CLEAR,** because there are no knots) comes from the heart of the tree and is the straightest, least warped and graded A. It's also the most expensive.

As you move down the grading ladder (B, C, D) the wood gets less perfect and therefore less expensive. There is also a step down from clear, which is called **COMMON**. Therefore B common is more likely to be warped and knotty than B clear.

Again let the project be your guide. Don't buy clear lumber if you're going to paint it—that's a waste of money. You won't mind the knots on shelves that are going to be painted, but the lumber does have to be straight.

Most lumberyards will allow you to pick out your own wood if you ask them, and it's something you should do. By choosing carefully, you won't end up with wood you can't use. Also, you might find some good boards in the cheaper grades.

PLYWOOD AND ALL THE REST—THE BASICS

There are lots of varieties of laminated boards. They're all made by gluing thin layers (or chunks) of wood together under heat and pressure and are sold in large sheets, usually 4 feet by 8 feet.

PLYWOOD

Plywood is one of the most common building materials used by professionals and do-it-yourselfers. The cheapest sheets are simply finished in a soft wood like pine and are used for general construction. The most expensive are finished in a very thin layer (veneer) of a hardwood like oak and are used to make furniture and cabinets.

Plywood is made in several thicknesses (anywhere from ⅛ inch to 1½ inches) but it's usually sold in 4 feet x 8 feet sheets. The most common thicknesses used are between ⅛ and ¾ inch. It's graded like board lumber from A to D. This refers to how many sides are finished and to what grade. For instance, A/A means both sides are perfect, which equals expensive. D/D means both sides are the bottom of the barrel, which equals cheap. A/C means one side is perfect and one side is average. Again, the project will determine the grade you choose.

PARTICLEBOARD

Particleboard is made from chips and chunks of wood that are formed and bonded together into sheets. Inexpensive, it's used for rough cabinet work, basic construction and flooring, anything that's not going to be seen.

HARDBOARD

Also called **MASONITE** (a friend of mine also calls it gorilla board because it's so heavy and smelly). Hardboard is made from softwood pulp that is mixed and rolled out in sheets. It's easy to work with, but wear a mask and goggles when you cut it because the dust is tough on the lungs. It's used underneath floor coverings to create a smooth surface and for cabinet backs, drawer bottoms and small sliding doors. It comes in 4 feet X 8 feet sheets although you can also get it as large as 6 feet X 16 feet. There are two kinds: tempered (stronger), which has one shiny side and one dull side, and untempered (weaker), which is dull on both sides.

When it's full of holes it's called pegboard, which is put on walls and uses hooks and hanging attachments to create a very economical, if not very fancy, form of vertical storage space.

FASTENERS—THE BASICS

NAILS

There still aren't many better ways to join things together as quickly and inexpensively as with good old-fashioned nails.

Common nails have heads and range from 1 to 6 inches in length. I don't know why but their length is designated in pennies—a 3 inch common for instance is called a 6 penny nail (6d). You can get a conversion chart at the hardware store until you get used to it.

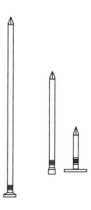

Finishing nails have tiny heads and are used when a nail must be driven below the surface of the material with a "nail set" to hide it. They range from 1 to 4 inches in length (but again are referred to in pennies).

Cut nails are made of steel and are flat instead of round. They are used to nail wood to masonry.

Cut flooring nails are flat as well, and are used to nail floorboards to joists.

Fluted masonry nails have spirals running down the shaft. They attach wood to concrete blocks or brick walls.

Duplex nails have two heads and are used when something needs to be nailed securely but not forever.

Brads are tiny nails for finishing work.

SCREWS

Screws are defined by length (in inches) and thickness, or gauge (a number from 1 to 20). Length is determined by the distance from the tip to the part of the head that will end up flush to the surface. The thicker the gauge the higher the number. Most common gauges in use are 3 through 10 and most screws fall into a range of length from ¼ to 6 inches. You'll find the largest variety of screws in gauges 6 through 12.

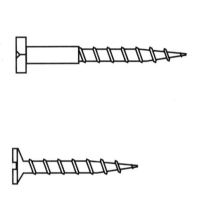

Screws join materials with incredible strength. In a lot of applications they've replaced nails, especially in do-it-yourself projects. All these screws come in the traditional slotted head and cross-slotted, or "Phillips," head design, but there are screws with special heads for specific jobs. Screws come in a wide range of shapes and sizes and have three basic head shapes:

- **Flat Head**—used when the screw must be flush to the surface or countersunk (meaning to drive the screw below the surface of the material to hide it).

- **Round Head**—used for materials that are too thin (less than ¼ inch) to countersink.

- **Oval Head**—a combination of flat and round head used when attaching metal to furniture.

SPECIALTY SCREWS—THE BASICS

Lag Bolts or Fag Screws are used when a strong connection is required, like attaching a gate to a fence, assembling a deck or putting together a picnic table. They have a square or hex head and are usually screwed in with a wrench. You have to drill a hole of a smaller diameter to set them in or you probably won't be able to tighten them down. Use a washer to prevent the head from sinking into the lumber as you tighten it.

SCREW HOOKS AND EYES—MULTITUDES OF USES

Self-Tapping Screws cut their own threads in the material as they are driven, making for a tight connection in sheet metal or plastic.

WALL MOUNTINGS AND ANCHORS—THE BASICS

Hanging things from walls used to be pretty hard, at least if you wanted them to stay up. But today there are fasteners available for almost any application and they're easy to put up in almost anything from brick to Sheetrock walls. And when you put something up it'll stay there.

You need to know the load you intend to place on anything you hang on a wall and choose the mounting device that is rated for the job. Check with the hardware store and read the manufacturer's instructions carefully.

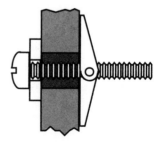

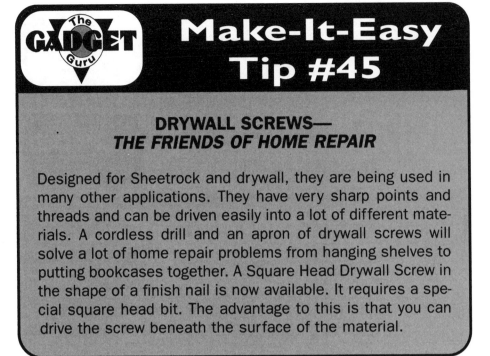

Make-It-Easy Tip #45

DRYWALL SCREWS—
THE FRIENDS OF HOME REPAIR

Designed for Sheetrock and drywall, they are being used in many other applications. They have very sharp points and threads and can be driven easily into a lot of different materials. A cordless drill and an apron of drywall screws will solve a lot of home repair problems from hanging shelves to putting bookcases together. A Square Head Drywall Screw in the shape of a finish nail is now available. It requires a special square head bit. The advantage to this is that you can drive the screw beneath the surface of the material.

WALL ANCHORS come in many shapes and sizes and are used in solid walls and in Sheetrock or hollow walls. You'll find Molded Plastic, Extruded Plastic, Fiber, Extruded Aluminum, and Threaded Metal Plugs made of aluminum. They all work by expanding into the hole when the screw or bolt is screwed in.

EXPANSION BOLTS consist of a bolt in a threaded expander. You drill the hole, insert the expansion bolt and tap it home. Then you tighten the bolt to expand the casing. Once it's tight you can remove the bolt, hang whatever you're hanging and re-set it. You can screw anything that's the right size, such as a hook, in the hole. They are very strong.

HOLLOW WALL MOUNTINGS are designed specifically for hollow walls. When inserted into the hole, the mechanism comes out the other side and expands against the back surface as the screw is tightened. You have to know the thickness of the wall so that the fastener you choose will go all the way through; otherwise it won't work.

Special Wall Plugs, Plastic Toggles and Collapsible Anchors all open behind the wall when the screw or bolt is turned.

Make-It-Easy Tip #46

UNFREEZING NUTS AND BOLTS

Too much force with a wrench on a frozen nut will blunt the edges and then it's nearly impossible to remove it without a dozen hacksaw blades or a stick of dynamite.

First take some penetrating oil. It's made to work its way into the threads and lubricate them. Wait a bit and try to loosen it. If the bolt has a slotted head use a screwdriver to hold it in place while you try to turn the nut. If it's square-headed use a crescent wrench to hold it. (Make sure you're turning it counterclockwise. Even the pros occasionally make the mistake of cranking a nut in the wrong direction.) Just remember—*Right is tight/Left is loose.*

If that doesn't do the job, use a propane torch or even a hair dryer to heat the nut briefly. The heat will loosen rust or paint and warm the oil, making it more efficient. Heat and repeat.

Stick with it and the nut should eventually come off. But if it doesn't, you might have to resort to a hacksaw or make it a professional's problem.

GRAVITY TOGGLES and **SPRING TOGGLES** both have arms or wings that catch against the interior wall. The weight of the wing on the gravity toggle causes it to fall after it's inserted. Spring toggles have spring-driven wings that pop open once they clear the hole on the other side. **NYLON STRAP TOGGLES** operate on the same principle.

ADHESIVES—THE BASICS

Nobody in the chemistry department has come up with a single glue that will literally hold anything to anything, but they're coming closer every day. The result is that there are enough different products on the market to deal with most of your gluing needs. Read the manufacturer's instructions carefully for warnings about fumes and instructions for proper use.

WOOD GLUES Everybody knows the familiar white or yellow Elmer's Glue bottles. Elmer's is made of polyvinyl acetates, or PVA. These glues are safe, effective and strong if used properly and can repair a lot of things around the house. Although the joint is solid in about thirty minutes it isn't completely bonded for about 24 hours. Both surfaces to be joined are coated and then nailed, screwed or clamped together. Extra glue that squeezes out should be cleaned away with a damp rag immediately because the glue won't take paint or stain.

CONTACT ADHESIVES are what hold materials like Formica to kitchen cabinets or countertops. The bond is extremely tight and also instant. The adhesive is rolled or brushed on both surfaces and allowed to dry. When the materials are pressed together, they're together forever.

FLOORING ADHESIVES are rubber resin or latex based, and bond a large variety of materials, like cork, tile and linoleum, to a large variety of subfloors. They have to be flexible enough to hold their own against the pressure of movement on the floor, as well as against variations in temperature, washing and spills.

METAL ADHESIVES are epoxy—resins so strong they're almost as solid as a weld. They can often be used to make an emergency plumbing repair. (See Part 4.)

KRAZY GLUE and its many competitors are cyanoacrylates and can cement almost anything to almost anything else. This, of course, includes your fingertips or anything else you touch. It doesn't work at all if you don't follow the directions or if you try to use it on something too big, since it's meant for small repairs.

The next few projects aren't as much about projects as they are about mastering some basic skills you're going to need to do carpentry and woodworking around the house. If you spend a little time learning how to hammer a nail, cut a board and drill a hole, you'll move on to more difficult projects quickly and safely.

MAKE-IT-EASY PRACTICE PROJECT #9-1
Hammering a Nail like a Pro

As with everything else in home repair you have to choose the right hammer for the job you're doing. Basically you want the weight of the tool to do most of the work. Sixteen ounce claw hammers drive big nails and finish hammers drive little nails. Pounding nails is an act of skill and to master it requires practice.

I think the hardest thing for a beginner to understand is that the weight of the hammer's head is what drives the nail. It's not as much a matter of strength as it is balance and accuracy. The power and accuracy comes from your wrist. Short swings with a lot of wrist are what you're looking for. The nail will go in just as fast and you'll be far less likely to mangle your thumbs.

Unless you're just banging a couple of boards together you also have to know when it's time to stop swinging and use a nail set to finish the job. The wood is a whole lot softer than the hammer and dents easily.

Make-It-Easy Tip #47

HOW NOT TO SPLIT A BOARD WHILE YOU'RE NAILING IT

A nail will most often go into the wood in the direction it's first set with the hammer. If you want it straight, set it straight; the same with an angle. Nailing through thin lumber, especially near the edges, can cause the board to split and ruin the piece. There are a couple of options. Drill a pilot hole smaller than the nail or blunt the point of the nail with your hammer before you swing away. Try rubbing a little soap or wax on the nail before you drive it. A little lubrication makes it go in easier.

Make-It-Easy Tip #48

The GADGET Guru

BE PREPARED—
SETTING UP A BASIC FIRST AID KIT

Even if you never pick up a hammer, having a well-stocked first aid kit around the house is as important as having working fire extinguishers and smoke detectors. And take it from me, no matter how careful a do-it-yourselfer you are, slivers, scratches, cuts, scrapes and gouges are inevitable when you're working on home projects. These are minor injuries to be sure but they still require tender loving care. You can purchase ready made first aid kits at the drugstore but make sure they include the following and restock items as you use them up.

I think it's also a good idea to keep a chart of antidotes and procedures in case of accidental poisoning or contact with hazardous materials. You can get one from the drugstore or hospital and sometimes from the local fire department or Red Cross.

Adhesive Tape
  (1, 2, 3 inch Rolls)
Antibiotic Ointment
Antiseptic Hand Cleaner
Aspirin or Analgesic
Band-Aids (Different Sizes)
Cotton Pads
Elastic Bandages
Eye Cup and Eye Wash
Flashlight and Batteries
Gauze Bandages (2 and 4
  inches)
Gauze Pads (4 x 4 inches)
Hydrogen-Peroxide 3%
  (Cleaning Wounds)

Ice Bag and Ice Pack
  (in Freezer)
Ipecac Syrup
  (for Accidental Poisoning)
Needles
Q-tips
Safety Pins
Scissors
Tongue Depressors
  (for Splints)
Triangular Bandage
  (Bandage or Sling)
Tweezers

![The Gadget Guru] **Make-It-Easy Tip #49**

WORKING WITH TINY NAILS

Brads and other ridiculously small nails are a pain in the neck, not to mention the fingers. They're impossible to hold. Slide the nail into the teeth of an old pocket comb, punch it through a piece of cardboard or hold it with your needle nose pliers. Works every time.

MAKE-IT-EASY PRACTICE PROJECT #9-2
Learning to Handle a Handsaw like a Pro

The basic techniques you'll learn as you master the handsaw will serve you well when you're ready to try a jigsaw or circular saw. And you'll learn a little bit about wood in the process.

A good cut on a piece of lumber is the result of a process that will become a habit. It involves several steps that become automatic. As when swinging a hammer you have to remember to let the saw do the work.

Level: Beginner
Tools: Handsaw * Combination square * Pencil
Materials: Scrap lumber (1 x 3, 1 x 6, 1 x 8 or whatever you've got around)
Also: A low bench

1) Measure and mark the piece of lumber you want to cut and set it securely on a sawhorse or low bench.

2) If you're right-handed, put your left knee up on the stock to hold it firmly in place and to get yourself out over the work for better leverage and balance.

3) Hold the saw with your fore-
finger pointing toward the blade.
This helps you keep the saw
in line and will produce a
straighter cut.

4) Start the cut by drawing the saw back toward you several times with
light strokes to establish the *kerf,* or cut.

5) Continue sawing with slow steady strokes and use the full length of
the blade. When you've almost cut through, move your left hand over
to hold the waste so your final strokes won't break off the last part of
the board.

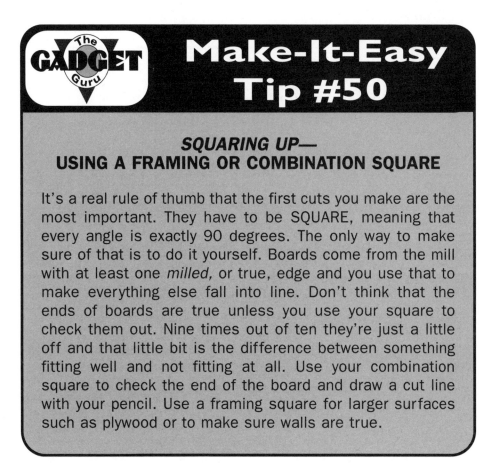

SQUARING UP—
USING A FRAMING OR COMBINATION SQUARE

It's a real rule of thumb that the first cuts you make are the
most important. They have to be SQUARE, meaning that
every angle is exactly 90 degrees. The only way to make
sure of that is to do it yourself. Boards come from the mill
with at least one *milled,* or true, edge and you use that to
make everything else fall into line. Don't think that the
ends of boards are true unless you use your square to
check them out. Nine times out of ten they're just a little
off and that little bit is the difference between something
fitting well and not fitting at all. Use your combination
square to check the end of the board and draw a cut line
with your pencil. Use a framing square for larger surfaces
such as plywood or to make sure walls are true.

GADGET The Guru

Make-It-Easy Tip #51

PUTTING A NEW SCREW IN AN EXISTING HOLE

Sometimes there's no alternative but to replace a screw in the same hole. But the reason you're replacing it is probably because it's loose. So, what do you do? First try a screw of a larger gauge (thicker) or one that is longer, but make sure it's not so long that it'll come through the other side. A second option is to drill the hole out to a larger size and tap in a piece of dowel that has been coated with carpenter's glue. You can also try filling the existing hole with wooden match sticks or toothpicks or stuff some steel wool into the opening.

MAKE-IT-EASY PRACTICE PROJECT #9-3
Using Electric Drills

An electric drill is probably the most versatile power tool in your box. Advances in battery technology have introduced powerful cordless models that rival the standard cord powered models for a lot of home repair projects. My personal collection consists of a heavy-duty ⅜ inch corded model that doubles as a hammer drill (the bit is pushed back and forth as it turns) for cutting into brick and masonry. With the proper attachments electric drills become screwdrivers, sanders, polishers, hedge trimmers, paint stirrers, jigsaws, pumps, metal grinders and much more. In fact, there are so many features available that you would do well to shop around before you buy.

Here are some basic things to consider when purchasng an electric drill.

• The *chuck* size of the drill is the limitation on the shaft size of bits you can use. A ⅜ inch chuck is more than adequate. Some chucks are self-tightening, meaning they don't need what's called a chuck key to tighten the bit. If you tend to lose things like I do, that's a major consideration.

• Don't buy anything that doesn't have a variable speed feature where finger pressure on the trigger of the drill controls the speed of the motor. Slower speeds produce more turning force (or torque) and higher speeds produce cleaner cuts in wood and soft materials.

• The trigger should have a locking device that will allow you to run the drill without having to keep pressing the trigger. This is valuable when you are using sanding or polishing features.

• Make sure the drill is reversible, meaning that the motor can turn in either direction. When you're using it as a screwdriver you'll want to be able to take screws out as well as put them in.

• Before you put down your money, hold the drill in your hand and make sure it feels balanced and comfortable.

• Get a carrying case if your drill doesn't come with one. It's a good way to keep track of bits and attachments.

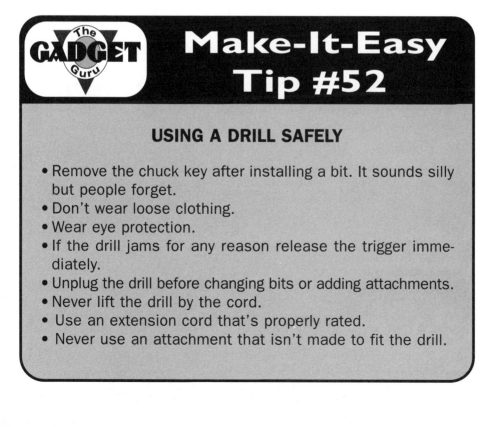

Make-It-Easy Tip #52

The Gadget Guru

USING A DRILL SAFELY

• Remove the chuck key after installing a bit. It sounds silly but people forget.
• Don't wear loose clothing.
• Wear eye protection.
• If the drill jams for any reason release the trigger immediately.
• Unplug the drill before changing bits or adding attachments.
• Never lift the drill by the cord.
• Use an extension cord that's properly rated.
• Never use an attachment that isn't made to fit the drill.

Spend some time trying out drills at the store until you find the one that has the features you want and is comfortable in your hand. Practice drilling holes of different sizes in scrap lumber. The hardest thing to learn is how to keep the drill straight up and down. It takes a little practice.

MAKE-IT-EASY PROJECT #9-4
Hang Some Cup Hooks in Your Kitchen

Hanging coffee cups from underneath a kitchen shelf is a great way to get additional storage space and a great way to begin learning to use your drill.

Level: Beginner
Tools: Electric drill * Drill bits * Tape measure * Pencil
Materials: Brass cup hooks (make sure the hook is big enough for your cups)

1) Decide where you want to hang the cups and how many will fit by measuring the length of the shelf and the approximate width of the cups. Use your tape measure and pencil to mark points for the cup hooks along the length of the shelf. Drill pilot holes at each mark with a bit that is smaller than the diameter of the screw at the end of the cup hook.

2) Screw in the hooks.

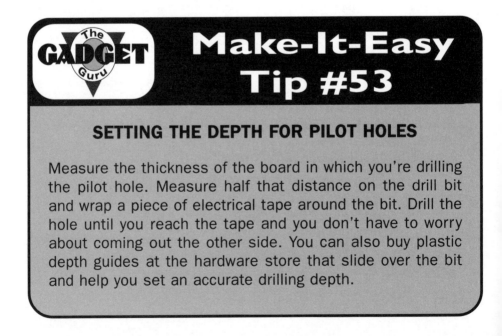

Make-It-Easy
Tip #53

SETTING THE DEPTH FOR PILOT HOLES

Measure the thickness of the board in which you're drilling the pilot hole. Measure half that distance on the drill bit and wrap a piece of electrical tape around the bit. Drill the hole until you reach the tape and you don't have to worry about coming out the other side. You can also buy plastic depth guides at the hardware store that slide over the bit and help you set an accurate drilling depth.

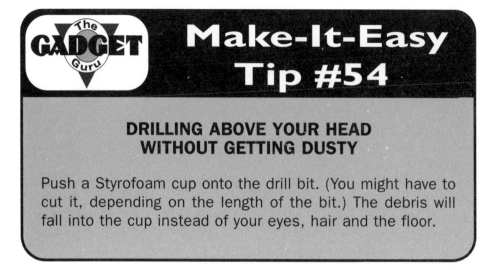

The most important part of hanging a picture is getting the right hardware for the job. The weight of the picture and the wall it will hang on will determine the size and style of the picture hook. Picture hangers come in packages that clearly state the weight they will support—trust them. Wallboard, wood and plaster walls are the easiest to deal with. The picture hanger, which comes with its own hardware, simply nails into the wall. If you're dealing with a brick or masonry wall you will have to use an anchor and a screw hook. (See p. 177.)

The weight will also determine the kind of wire you use to mount it. Pictures are most often hung with nylon fishing line or what's called picture wire. Picture wire is similar to some electrical wire; it's braided to make it extremely flexible and easy to work with. The hardware people can help you get wire that's right for your picture. It wraps through the screw eye on the picture frame and back on itself so that the length can be adjusted. Picture wire is easily cut with wire clippers.

HANGING A PICTURE WITH TWO HOOKS

Level: Beginner
Tools: Hammer * Carpenter's level * Tape measure * Pencil
Materials: Picture hangers * Wall anchors and screw hooks (if necessary)
Also: Electric drill * Masonry bit * Carpenter's awl

The size of the picture will determine how many hooks you need to hang. Pictures over 28 to 30 inches long will be better supported by two hooks. If you use two hooks they have to be mounted level to each other on the wall.

The hooks should be set so they're about 6 to 10 inches from the outside edge of the frame when the picture is on the wall.

It's easy to do.

1) Once you determine the height and center position of the picture on the wall, measure half the distance from the center position, make a mark and put up the hanger.

2) Place your carpenter's level on top of the mounted hook and measure over to the correct point on the other side. Level it off and make a mark. Mount the second hanger.

MAKE-IT-EASY PROJECT #9-6
Hang Up Your Mops and Brooms on a Wallboard Wall

It's easy to get your brooms and mops off the floor and onto the wall.

Level: Beginner
Tools: Electric drill * Electric screwdriver * Masonry bit * Tape measure * Pencil * Carpenter's level * Carpenter's awl * Hammer
Materials: Metal utility rack with hooks * Screws (if none come with the rack) * Plastic anchors (if you're mounting it on a wallboard)

1) Decide where you want to mount the rack and how high you want it off the ground by measuring the longest broom and adding about a foot. Mark the point with your pencil. Punch a tiny guide hole for the masonry bit so you don't have to worry about the drill "walking" as you

drill the hole. Drill the hole in the wallboard making sure it's straight and not at an angle. Tap the anchor gently into the hole with your hammer until it's flush with the wall.

NOTE: Masonry bits are specially designed for drilling holes in brick, concrete block and wallboard. The size of the bit depends on the size of the anchor you're going to use. The size of the anchor depends on the size of the screw that is required for the piece you're hanging. When you pick out the rack you're going to hang, ask your hardware person to give you the right size anchors and masonry bits for the job.

2) Mount the rack and put the screw into the anchor until it's just tight but still moves easily. Set your carpenter's level on the rack and raise or lower it until the bubble shows its level. Mark the spot for the other hole. Swing the rack out of the way and set the second anchor as in Step 1. Swing the rack back into place and put in the second screw. Tighten both until they are secure. Be careful not to over-tighten, or the anchor will begin to turn and come out of the wall.

MAKE-IT-EASY PROJECT #9-7
Make a Coat Rack

Making a coat rack is a good project for putting together several basic skills. You have to cut a board, screw on some hooks and mount it on the wall.

Level: Beginner
Tools: Handsaw, jigsaw or circular saw * Combination square *
            Hammer * Tape measure * Pencil * Electric drill with bits *
            Electric screwdriver * Carpenter's awl * Carpenter's level
Materials: Brass coat hooks with screws * 1 x 4 clear pine * Plastic
            anchors * Screws * Sandpaper * Paint or stain

1) Decide how long the coat rack will be and how many hooks you want to use. You should figure to mount the hooks at least 6 to 8 inches apart. Use the combination square to mark a true line at the end of the board. Make the cut, then measure down the board to the desired length. Mark the second cut with your square and saw away.

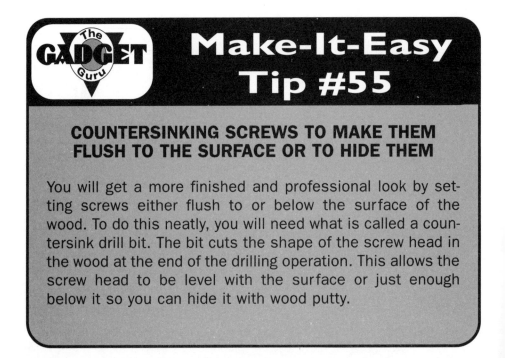

Make-It-Easy
Tip #55

COUNTERSINKING SCREWS TO MAKE THEM FLUSH TO THE SURFACE OR TO HIDE THEM

You will get a more finished and professional look by setting screws either flush to or below the surface of the wood. To do this neatly, you will need what is called a countersink drill bit. The bit cuts the shape of the screw head in the wood at the end of the drilling operation. This allows the screw head to be level with the surface or just enough below it so you can hide it with wood putty.

The GADGET Guru
Make-It-Easy Tip #56

WHAT TO DO WHEN YOU CAN'T UNSCREW

Inevitably a screw that you need to come out won't. It's stuck, it's frozen, it's jammed—whatever the reason, it won't budge and you need to get it out. Before you thrash around like King Kong with a screwdriver take a deep breath and look at the problem. Too much force and you might strip the screw head, making it impossible to turn the screw. Patience, patience, patience.

• If the slot of the screw is filled with paint or plaster, chip it out with the edge of your screwdriver and tap the head gently to loosen the paint around the edges. Use your carpenter's awl or a finish nail to pry paint out of a Phillips head.

• Make sure the blade of your screwdriver fits into the slot. If it's too big and you don't have a smaller one, use a hacksaw to gently widen the opening.

• Put the screwdriver in the screw slot and tap it gently. Sometimes the vibrations will loosen it enough so you can unscrew it.

• If the screw is halfway out and stuck, try screwing it back in a few turns and then try taking it out. Squirt a little penetrating oil around the screw and wait a while for it to do its work. Try it again. A little in, a little out, it may free itself. Or take your channel locks and clamp them firmly on the screw head. It will probably give you enough leverage to get it out.

If all else fails, ask your hardware person about specially tempered bits that can drill the old screw out of the hole.

2) Sand the board until it's smooth. Space the hooks evenly along the board, making sure they are centered. Leave space on either end for the mounting holes. Mark the holes for the hooks and drill pilots. Next, choose a wood bit that is slightly larger than the screws you're going to use to mount the coat rack. Drill the mounting holes at each end of the board—they should go all the way through. If you're going to paint or stain the coat rack, now's the time to do it.

3) When you've finished painting or staining, use your electric screwdriver to mount the hooks on the board. Hang the coat rack on the wall following the steps you used to put up the broom rack in project #9-6.

NOTE: Make sure the mounting screws are long enough to go through the board and into the full length of the anchor. The combination of the depth of the board and the length of the anchor will determine the length of the screw.

MAKE-IT-EASY PROJECT #9-8
Hanging Standard and Bracket Shelving on a Wallboard Wall

Adding shelving to a laundry room, office, garage or anyplace else in your house is easy to do, and the extra space is always welcome. I personally love to put up shelves; it's very satisfying work. I think the simplest systems for beginners to start out with is **STANDARD AND BRACKET.**

Standard and bracket systems consist of standards, which are slotted metal channels of varying lengths, and shelf brackets with hooks that lock into the slots. The slots are spaced up and down the length of the standard to make the shelving fully adjustable. The standards have mounting holes drilled every 12 inches to fix them on the wall.

Proper spacing of the standards is important. If they are too far apart, the shelves will sag. The thicker the shelf material, the more distance you can have between the standards. Most shelving is made of 1 inch stock. The rule of thumb is that a 1 inch shelf needs support every 36 inches to prevent sagging. The supports should be inset from the ends at least 6 to 8 inches to balance the load.

In this project we'll put up four 10 inch shelves, 35 inches long, on a wallboard wall. Other wall surfaces, like brick or concrete, will require different styles of fasteners but the steps will be the same.

Level: Beginner
Tools: Drill with masonry bit * Carpenter's level * Hammer * Pencil
            * Carpenter's awl * Tape measure * Handsaw (or circular,
            or jigsaw) * Combination square * Electric screwdriver
Materials: 1 X 10 X 12 feet clear pine board * Two metal standards 48
            inches long * Eight 10 inch shelf brackets * Eight 2 inch
            plastic anchors with 2 inch screws
Also: An assistant

1) Measure, square and cut four 35 inch shelves from the 1 X 10 X 12. Don't measure all four at once. Measure one, cut it and then do the next. Sand the edges until smooth and clean. If they're going to be painted or stained do it now and then move on to mount the standards.

2) The first decisions are where the shelves are going to go and how high you want the tallest shelf. Once you've decided that, the next step is to mount the first standard. Place the standard against the wall so that the highest point is at least 6 inches above the top shelf. Hold the standard against the wall and use the carpenter's awl to make a mark on the wall through one of the middle mounting holes. Any one of them will do. Set the standard aside and punch the mark a little deeper so you have a guide for the drill bit.

3) Using the correct masonry bit, drill the first hole. This is where a variable speed model comes in handy—by starting at a slower speed you have more control of the drill and can make a more accurate hole. Tap the plastic anchor gently into the hole until it's flush. Feed a screw through the same hole in the standard which you used to mark the wall. Put the screw into the anchor and screw it in gently until the standard is against the wall but still able to move.

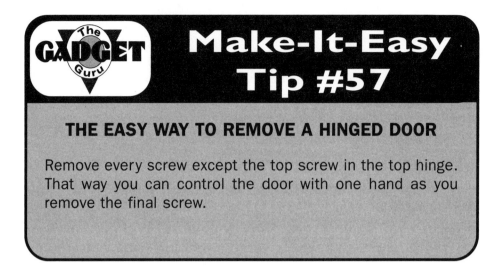

THE EASY WAY TO REMOVE A HINGED DOOR

Remove every screw except the top screw in the top hinge. That way you can control the door with one hand as you remove the final screw.

4) Take your level and hold it against the standard, adjust the standard until it's level and carefully mark the rest of the holes. Shift the standard aside. Drill and fit the remaining anchors. Shift the standard back into place and screw it in.

5) Now you need to do a little math to get the position for the second standard. The shelves are 35 inches long, and remember that they need to overhang at least 6 inches on each end. Subtract 12 from 35, and you know that the second standard has to be approximately 23 inches from the one that's already on the wall. Measure over and make a mark. Hook a bracket to the mounted standard. Place the loose standard next to it and hook a bracket in the same holes as the mounted one.

6) At this point you'll need to call in your assistant. Move the loose standard over to the 23 inch mark. While you hold the standard on the mark have your assistant set the shelf on the brackets. Place the level on the shelf. Adjust the shelf until it's level and mark your first hole in the wall with the awl. Mount the second standard the same way you did the first one. Hook the brackets on both sides and put your shelves in place.

NOTE: Some brackets may need to be tapped into place gently with a hammer.

Step back and take a look at your handy work. You're finished.

MAKE-IT-EASY PROJECT #9-9
Stopping Squeaks in Your Floors and Staircases

Right up there with leaking and dripping faucets are squeaky floors and stairs. Squeaks occur when changes in humidity cause the wood to shrink or expand and also from just general wear and tear. The noise you hear is pieces of wood, such as the subfloor and the finished floor that lays on top of it, rubbing together. The subfloor may have also separated from the joists. In staircases, treads (what you walk on) and risers (what carry the treads to the next level) can move apart.

There are some things you can do to stop these floor "mice." You'll need some or all of the following tools and materials depending on what you do.

Level: Beginner
Tools: Electric drill and wood bits * Hammer * Screwdriver * Tape measure * Circular saw or handsaw * Combination square * Nail set * Mat
Materials: Wooden shims. (A shim is a piece of wood that looks like a roofing shingle. It is used as a wedge to fill in gaps between two pieces of wood) * Flooring nails (spiral shanked) * Common nails * Wood screws * White or yellow wood glue * Wood putty * Wood the same dimensions as your floor joists (usually 2 x 12 or 2 x 10 pine) * 2 x 2 pine (for cleat blocks—see p. 185)
Also: An assistant for some of the following steps

FLOORS—WORKING FROM BELOW

1) If the squeaks are on the first floor and the basement doesn't have a finished ceiling, the first line of attack is to try driving shims between the joists and the subfloor. Have your assistant walk on the floor above while you watch for movement. When you find the culprits, coat a shim with glue and use your hammer to drive it between the subfloor and the joist.

Make-It-Easy Tip #58

DON'T GOUGE THE FURNITURE

Use your file to round the edges of the putty knife. That way you won't mar or scratch the surface you've worked so hard to restore.

2) If the noise is coming from boards between the joists, measure the distance between the joists and cut a piece of wood to fit or "bridge" the distance between the joists. Drive it up between the joists with your hammer until it is firmly against the subfloor and nail it in place through the joists.

WORKING ABOVE THE FLOOR

You'll have to work from above whenever there's a finished ceiling below.

3) If you have hardwood floors you'll find that they will sometimes lift up from the subfloor or joists and need to be reconnected. Use your electric drill with a bit that is a smaller size than the spiraled flooring nails and drill pilot holes at an angle through the floorboards. Drive the spiral flooring nails into the flooring

below and finish them below the surface with your nailset. Fill the holes with wood putty.

4) If you have carpet on the floor, pull it back to expose the sub-floor. Drive nails or screws through the floor into the joists.

STAIRCASES—WORKING FROM ABOVE AND BELOW

1) If the squeak is coming from the front of the tread, drill a pilot hole at an angle like you did for the floor. Drive and set the flooring nails. Have someone stand on the tread while you do it to get a good fit. Fill the holes with wood putty.

2) If the squeak comes from the back of the tread, coat a shim with glue and drive it between the tread and riser. Wipe away excess glue with a damp rag, and when it's dry, trim the excess away with a mat knife.

3) If you can get underneath the staircase you can attach **CLEAT BLOCKS** to the tread and riser. A cleat makes a much stronger connection between the tread and the riser, and since it's underneath the staircase you don't have to worry about drilling holes in the top. Cut a 2 X 2 to a length long enough to fix the squeak. Drill pilot holes through

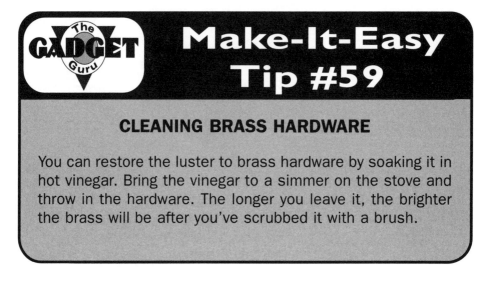

Make-It-Easy Tip #59

CLEANING BRASS HARDWARE

You can restore the luster to brass hardware by soaking it in hot vinegar. Bring the vinegar to a simmer on the stove and throw in the hardware. The longer you leave it, the brighter the brass will be after you've scrubbed it with a brush.

the cleat in the directions of both the treads and risers. Coat the cleat with glue and screw it into place. (Make sure the wood screws aren't too long; otherwise they'll come out through the top of the steps.)

CHAPTER TEN

Keeping Things Running—
Maintaining Major
and Small Appliances

*I*f it ain't broke, don't fix it is one of my favorite sayings. There's a little variation that I like even better: *If you take care of it, it's a lot less likely to break.* That has never been more true than it is with your home appliances, from your dryer right down to your electric toothbrush. Preventive maintenance is how you really save money in the long run.

The manuals that come with every appliance are a blessing for the beginning do-it-yourselfer. First, they give detailed maintenance instructions designed to keep the unit in tip-top shape. Second, by doing the maintenance these manuals recommend, you learn about how the appliance works, and that'll help give you the skills to actually fix a lot of things yourself.

But first things first. The fact that I'm busy all the time doesn't fool me a bit. At heart, I'm basically a lazy man and the first thing I do when I've got a problem with an appliance is check the warranty. If it's covered I call the service man. Not just because it's easier but because if I try to fix something that's under warranty and still have to take it in, I may have voided the agreement between myself and the manufacturer. I suggest you take the time to read the warranty that comes with every appliance you buy so you know what's covered and for how long.

If it's not covered, however, I take a look at the problem and see if I can fix it myself. There are several things I consider when I'm thinking about fixing my appliances.

• Does the manufacturer recommend that the product be serviced only by a professional because of potential risk to the repairer?

• Some appliances, especially small ones, are often cheaper to replace than to fix. Many are even sealed in such a way that it's impossible to get to working parts.

• Large appliances like dryers, stoves or dishwashers are often easier to work on than smaller ones. They're built to be repaired and maintained. In fact, that's a good point to think about when purchasing a new appliance. You may want to ask the salesperson what type of repairs can be made without a service call.

• Do I have the skills necessary to do the repair job? Taking things apart and putting them back together is a process of trial-and-error and remembering your mistakes so you don't repeat them.

• Have I prepared myself to tackle the job? Read the manual? Made a plan? Got the tools and materials together? Given myself time to finish the project?

When I take anything apart, I'm very careful to watch what I'm doing and remember how things are attached to each other. If necessary, I make notes, draw a picture or even take a snap shot with my instant camera. I keep track of parts and label any wires so I know exactly where they go. I also remind myself to be patient when I'm trying to snap the widget back into place, telling myself that I got it off so it has to go back on.

And finally, I make good use of those 800 numbers in the instruction manuals when I have a question or need some advice.

Make-It-Easy Tip #60

BE YOUR OWN EXTENDED SERVICE CONTRACT

Extended service contracts, especially for electronic items and small appliances, are one of my pet peeves. You know what I'm talking about: you buy a stereo and the salesman tells you that for an additional fee it'll be fixed free for the next five years or whatever. It might sound good at the time, but for the most part I think it's money down the drain. Especially if the company that manages the service contract goes out of business, which happened once to me.

Quality control is so high these days that, in my experience, if a product is a lemon it'll break down well within the first 90 days. If that's the case you just return it and get a new one. But, if a TV set, for instance, works for the first three months it's probably going to work for years; by buying a service contract you're just gambling that it's going to break down before the contract runs out. Be sure to ask how much time (after the purchase) you will have to make a decision regarding the extended warranty. If it's a television, for example, and they give you 60 to 90 days, you surely will want to wait to see if it is giving you any warning signals that it might be a lemon before purchasing the extended warranty.

Also, be sure to ask what the standard warranty is on the product and the procedures needed for repair. Do they do the repair on site? Will you have to haul it to a factory service center? Will you have to ship it to a third world country? Who pays the freight? Will the retailer give you a loaner unit while yours is being repaired? Do they pay for parts and labor or just the parts?

My alternative is to take a portion of the money I would have spent on a contract and put it in my savings account. If something breaks down and isn't covered by warranty, I've got a little set aside for the repair, and if it doesn't I'm earning the interest on my money, not the service company.

TOOLS OF THE TRADE—Appliances

A lot of the tools you need to repair and maintain appliances are the same ones you use on electrical projects. If you've been building your basic tool box you've already got most of the things you'll need to fix a toaster or replace the switch in a refrigerator.

- Tools You'll Use from Your Basic Kit

Adjustable Wrench	Flashlight
Allen Wrenches	Mat Knife
Putty Knife	Electrical Pliers
Screwdrivers	Needle Nose Pliers
Slip Joint Pliers	Power Drill and Bits
Circuit Tester	Slotted Screwdrivers
Claw Hammer	Phillips Screwdrivers
Continuity Tester	Tape Measure
Electrician's Tape	Wire Strippers

MORE TOOLS OF THE TRADE

Here are some specialty tools that you'll need to work on appliances.

AUTOMOTIVE POINT FILE
A thin file used to clean and set the points on spark plugs, the point file is also excellent for cleaning electrical contacts.

CONTACT CLEANER Contact cleaner is a solvent that gets rid of dirt and corrosion from electrical contacts without damaging surrounding parts. It comes in an aerosol can with a plastic nozzle for getting into tight places.

NUT DRIVERS Nut drivers are special screwdrivers that fit over different sized nuts. They come in sets to fit most standard nuts.

TORX SCREWDRIVER A specialty screwdriver with a star shaped head. Torx screws are often found inside small appliances.

VOLT-OHM METER A volt-ohm meter measures voltage and resistance. It also tests for grounding and continuity. A very fancy and complicated looking tool but very easy to use and necessary for working on many appliances. Get a model with a digital readout; it's more accurate. Read the instructions carefully for safety tips.

VOLTAGE PROBE The voltage probe, which looks like a pen, is another version of your circuit tester, but it's easier to use for some applications such as testing outlets because you don't have to stick the probe inside. Just hold it near what you want to test, and it will either light up or make a noise if voltage is present.

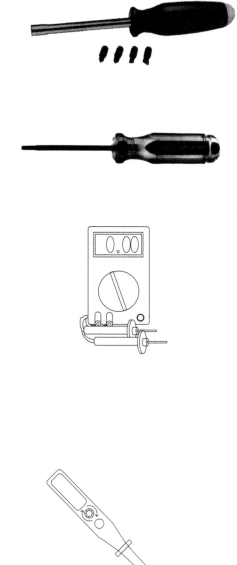

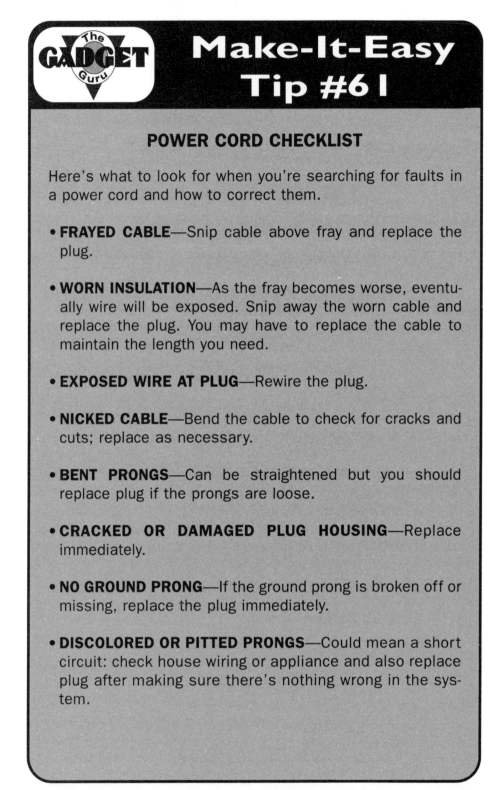

The GADGET Guru

Make-It-Easy Tip #61

POWER CORD CHECKLIST

Here's what to look for when you're searching for faults in a power cord and how to correct them.

- **FRAYED CABLE**—Snip cable above fray and replace the plug.

- **WORN INSULATION**—As the fray becomes worse, eventually wire will be exposed. Snip away the worn cable and replace the plug. You may have to replace the cable to maintain the length you need.

- **EXPOSED WIRE AT PLUG**—Rewire the plug.

- **NICKED CABLE**—Bend the cable to check for cracks and cuts; replace as necessary.

- **BENT PRONGS**—Can be straightened but you should replace plug if the prongs are loose.

- **CRACKED OR DAMAGED PLUG HOUSING**—Replace immediately.

- **NO GROUND PRONG**—If the ground prong is broken off or missing, replace the plug immediately.

- **DISCOLORED OR PITTED PRONGS**—Could mean a short circuit: check house wiring or appliance and also replace plug after making sure there's nothing wrong in the system.

REPAIRING AND MAINTAINING YOUR IRON

An electric iron has a powerful heating element and therefore puts a heavy demand on your system. That's the reason most manufacturers don't recommend using an extension cord. I agree. Set up your ironing board close to an outlet so you won't need one.

If you're having problems with your iron, start with simple things first. Check the circuits to make sure you aren't overloading. If overloading isn't the problem, then you've got a fault in the iron itself or a bad power cord.

When you use an iron you put a lot of stress on the cord, and you should inspect it frequently for frays and cracks. A frayed or broken cord can cause any number of problems including slow heating and low temperatures.

If your electric iron is tripping the circuit breaker or you receive a shock when you touch it, disconnect it and look for obvious problems with plugs and cords. If nothing is clearly wrong, the problem may be in the iron's circuit board, a problem which needs professional attention.

MAKE-IT-EASY PROJECT #10-1
Cleaning Your Iron

Even if your home has a water softener, minerals are still present in the water and they'll build up in your steam iron over time. The best all over maintenance for your iron is to keep it clean and to use distilled water to make steam.

Level: Beginner
Tools: Pipe cleaners * Fine sewing needle * Sponge * Very fine steel wool
Materials: Iron cleaning solution * Mild detergent

1) Use the pipe cleaners to gently clean the steam vents on the soleplate.

2) Use the sewing needle to clean the spray nozzle. Be very careful not to enlarge the opening. It could cause a leak.

3) Use the sponge and mild detergent to clean the soleplate. Rinse with clean water and dry. Don't immerse the iron in water.

4) If the soleplate is scratched or rough, use very fine steel wool to smooth it over. Work only in one direction and remove all the steel wool fibers when you're done. If the iron has a non-stick soleplate, follow manufacturer's instructions for cleaning.

5) Flush out the tank and chamber with a commercial cleaning solution. Place the iron on a metal rack over a pan. Fill with the cleaning solution and run the iron until dry. Repeat until no sediment comes out and then flush with distilled water to clean out the solution.

MAKE-IT-EASY PROJECT #10-2
Changing the Power Cord on Your Iron

Level: Beginner
Tools: Screwdriver * Continuity tester
Materials: Replacement cord (if necessary)

1) Unplug the iron and remove the screw on the backplate. Lift off the backplate and set it aside.

2) The wires are usually attached by screws to terminals or wire connectors. Take a mental picture of how everything looks and unhook the wires. There is very likely to be a strain relief fitting of some kind that will have to be disassembled as well. Remove the cord.

3) Use the continuity tester to check the plug and cord. Put the alligator clip onto one of the wires and touch the probe to one of the prongs. The light will come on if the wire is good, and you will know which prong corresponds to which wire. Test the other prong and the other wire; if the light comes on, the wire is good. If the light doesn't come on, the power cord needs to be replaced.

If the cord checks out, then the problem is in the iron and you should take it in for service.

MAKE-IT-EASY PROJECT #10-3
Checking the Temperature Setting on Your Iron

If your iron doesn't seem to be heating properly you can check the temperature setting and see if the thermostat needs to be recalibrated by your service people.

Level: Beginner
Tools: Oven thermometer * Coffee can * Metal pot

1) Turn the iron to the lowest steam setting and place it upside down in a metal cooking pot. Place an oven thermometer on the soleplate and cover it with the coffee can. Wait approximately five minutes and remove the can (remember—it's hot!). The oven thermometer should

be somewhere between 220 and 280 degrees. If not, the thermostat needs to be reset by a professional.

COMMON IRON PROBLEMS AND SOLUTIONS

1) IRON WON'T HEAT

- Make sure the temperature selector is on.
- Make sure the outlet works.
- Make sure the power cord and plug are working properly.
- Check to see if the thermostat is blocked or faulty.

2) IRON HEATS BUT WON'T STEAM

- Make sure there's water in the chamber, the steam button is on and the temperature selector is on steam settings.
- Make sure the steam vents aren't clogged.
- Make sure the steam chamber isn't clogged.
- Make sure the steam valve isn't clogged or broken.

3) NOT ENOUGH HEAT/TOO MUCH HEAT

- Check the power cord and plug.
- See if the thermostat needs calibration or is broken.

4) NO SPRAY

- Make sure the spray nozzle isn't clogged.

5) LEAKING AND SPITTING

- Make sure the tank isn't too full.
- Check that the temperature setting is correct. If the setting is correct on the dial, then thermostat needs to be recalibrated.
- Make sure the steam valve isn't broken.
- Make sure the steam chamber or water tank isn't cracked.
- Check all vents and nozzles for clogs.

6) IRON STICKS TO FABRIC

- Make sure the temperature setting is correct.
- Make sure the soleplate is clean.

7) IRON STAINS FABRIC

- Make sure the soleplate is clean.
- Make sure the water in the tank is clean.
- Make sure your water is not too hard. (Use distilled water.)

REPAIRING AND MAINTAINING YOUR BLENDER

MAKE-IT-EASY PROJECT # 10-4
Replacing or Repairing the Switch Mechanism in Your Blender

The problems with blenders are usually in the motor and/or the switches. That makes sense because that's about all there is to them mechanically. The motor should be repaired or replaced by a professional. But, if one of the switches isn't working, it could simply be dirty or it could be defective. Either way it's an easy fix.

Level: Beginner
Tools: Screwdriver * Mat knife * Volt-ohm meter
Materials: Contact cleaner

1) Unplug the blender and set it up on a work area. Test the switches with the volt-ohm meter as follows. Turn the on/off switch on. Set the volt meter to the setting RX1 scale. Clip the probes to the prongs on the plug. Press each switch and check the digital readout. Low ohms indicate that the switch is good. The infinity symbol means that the switch is faulty or dirty.

2) Look at the manual to see how the switch plate is removed. Generally you have to remove the screws that hold the base plate in place. Pull the base plate away.

3) Take the mat knife and carefully peel away the decorative covering to reveal the top screws that hold it in place. Remove the screws that hold the bottom in place. They are located inside the unit.

4) Peel away the decorative covering to reveal the screws that hold the switch mechanism in place.

5) Label the switch wires before you remove them so you can put them back in the same place. Use your screwdriver to slide the spade lug connectors off the connections. Don't pull them off by the wires; you may damage them.

Spray the electrical contact cleaner into switch openings and clean the connector pins.

6) Reconnect the switches and test again with the volt meter. If you still have problems you'll have to replace the switch mechanism. This is a simple matter of buying an exact replacement and sliding the labeled spade lugs on their proper connections. Reassemble and make a strawberry shake.

Make-It-Easy Tip #62

The GADGET Guru

A LITTLE STEREO SLEUTHING

Electronic appliances like stereos and televisions are complex pieces of equipment. Not so much because they have lots of moving parts but because of the circuit boards. They can sometimes be difficult to take apart and even dangerous to work on. If you mess around without knowing what you're doing, you could hurt yourself or at the very least void the warranty. Sometimes it's cheaper and easier to replace electronic gear than it is to get it fixed. Still, it's worth finding out if an expensive piece of equipment can be repaired before you exercise your wallet for a new one.

Here are some things you can do to maintain a stereo system and to isolate problems before you take it to a service center. Many of the problems with a stereo can be traced to connections and cables.

- Keep the components clean.
- The most common problem with receivers is oxidation of electrical contacts. Use a pencil eraser to clean jacks and cable pins regularly. Use your contact cleaner to clean jack inputs and speaker terminals.
- If the speakers hum make sure all the connections are tight and that the grounding wire is connected to the proper terminal on the back of the receiver, or try hooking the ground to the screw in the plate of an electrical outlet. If possible, plug the components into an outlet of their own.
- If a speaker isn't playing and the connections are clean and tight, the problem is likely to be in the speaker wires. Check the wires for continuity. If they are damaged, replace them. The longer the run to the speaker the beefier the wire size should be. The last thing to do is connect the silent speaker to the other speaker's wires. If it works, the problem is in the receiver. If it doesn't, then the speaker itself is faulty.

REPAIRING AND MAINTAINING ELECTRIC FANS

Window or box fans are about as simple as it gets—a blade mounted on the shaft of a motor. Second only to an exhaust fan mounted in the attic, they do the most efficient job of moving air out of the house. Oscillating fans are the choice for circulating air in individual rooms.

The most common problem with both types is the noise that comes from the blades being out of alignment because they are bent, broken or cracked. Metal blades can be realigned on either fan. But often plastic blades must be replaced. Clean the fan blades regularly, as buildup of dirt and grime can cause them to get out of alignment and put stress on the motor.

Make-It-Easy Tip #63

STOPPING BANGING GRILLS AND BLADE GUARDS

If the blade guards or grills rattle and the clips or screws can't be tightened, try sliding a piece of cardboard between the body and the grill. Sometimes it works.

MAKE-IT-EASY PROJECT #10-5
Window Fan Maintenance

Level: Beginner
Tools: Screwdriver • Ruler
Materials: Sponge • Mild detergent • Rags • Vacuum cleaner with brush or crevice tool

1) Stick the crevice tool onto your vacuum cleaner and clean the grill.

2) The grills of the fan are secured with either screws or plastic clips. Unplug the fan, lay it down on a work surface and remove these fasteners. Keep a container handy to hold the screws. If the grills are really dirty, clean them with soap and water before you put the fan back together.

3) If the blades are simply dirty, clean them with soap and water but don't get water into the motor. If the blades need realignment, remove them. The blades are usually secured in one of three ways:

• **FRICTION FIT**—Lay the fan down and grab the blades from below and lift off slowly.

• **SCREW MOUNTED**—Take out the screw and remove the blades.

• **C–CLIP**—Pry off with a screwdriver. As a safety precaution, wear your eye protection.

4) Lay the blades on a flat surface. An edge of each blade should touch the working surface. Use the ruler to check each blade at its highest point. If this measurement varies by more than ¼ inch, try to realign them by bending each blade until an edge touches the surface. If that doesn't work replace them.

5) While you've got the fan apart you should lubricate the motor if required. The manual will provide the information you need about how to do it and what grade oil to use.

6) If you're replacing the blades slide the new set on the shaft and resecure it. Rotate the blade to make sure it's turning with the shaft.

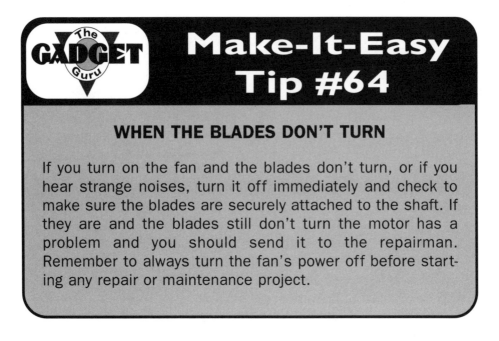

WHEN THE BLADES DON'T TURN

If you turn on the fan and the blades don't turn, or if you hear strange noises, turn it off immediately and check to make sure the blades are securely attached to the shaft. If they are and the blades still don't turn the motor has a problem and you should send it to the repairman. Remember to always turn the fan's power off before starting any repair or maintenance project.

MAKE-IT-EASY PROJECT #10-6
Oscillating Fan Maintenance

Oscillating fans develop problems in the pivot mechanism because the gears will eventually wear out. The pivot assembly should be replaced by a service center. But make sure it doesn't cost more than a new fan.

The blade guards are usually secured with clips which are easy to remove. The blade is secured with a spinner nut that screws onto the shaft. It is threaded to turn in the opposite direction from what you're used to (clockwise) so the nut won't spin off while the fan is turning.

Remove the nut and pull off the blades, clean them and check alignment with your ruler. Replace if necessary. Clean the blade guard and reassemble.

REPAIRING AND MAINTAINING YOUR REFRIGERATOR

We really have to remember that things were never intended to last forever, and no matter how bulky and solid a refrigerator or freezer may seem, it's like everything else—occasionally it needs a little love, affection and personal attention.

Here are some maintenance tips for keeping your refrigerator in good condition.

• At least once, but preferably twice, a year clean the condenser coils. They're located either underneath or behind the unit. Use the crevice tool on your vacuum cleaner to suck out the dust and anything else that may have found its way back there.

• Clean the gaskets around the refrigerator frequently to remove food particles. (Do the same with your microwave oven.)

Make-It-Easy Tip #65

KEEPING TRACK OF HARDWARE— *AN ALTERNATIVE*

A saucer or can is a great place to keep screws and such while you're working on something, but there's another trick that's even safer. Tear off a strip of masking tape and stick the screws and washers or whatever to the adhesive side.

• Flush the drainage system on your self-defrosting refrigerator. Check your manual for the position of the plugs that cover the drain holes. They should be at the bottom of both the freezer and refrigerator sections. Pull them out, and if necessary, unclog them with a pipe cleaner. Finish off by flushing the system using a turkey baster filled with warm water and a little ammonia to kill the algae. Dump the drain pan.

• If you find water collecting under your refrigerator, it's possible that the drain pan needs replacing or that the drain hose (if you have one) leaks. Slow leaks will become very expensive propositions if they're not stopped. The damage to the floor will eventually result in a major renovation project. Call in a professional to check the drain system.

MAKE-IT-EASY PROJECT #10-7
Leveling Your Refrigerator

Modern refrigerators have leveling screws or legs in the front. It's important that the refrigerator be level for it to work properly.

Level: Beginner
Tools: Screwdriver * Carpenter's level
Materials: Block of 2 x 4 pine

1) Check the unit with the level on the front and on the side. The refrigerator should be *plumb* (vertical) on the side. While setting the unit to tip slightly front to back, make sure the doors stay closed because an open door can also adversely affect the operation of an icemaker.

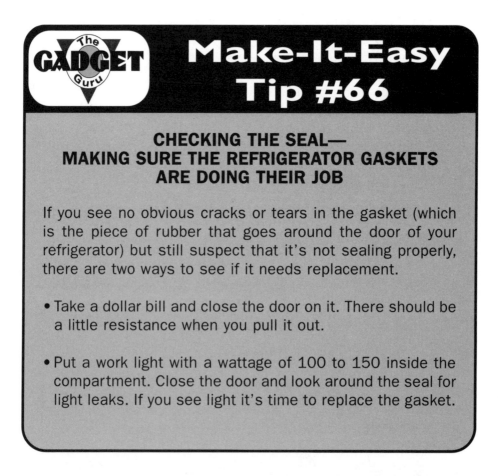

Make-It-Easy
Tip #66

CHECKING THE SEAL—
MAKING SURE THE REFRIGERATOR GASKETS
ARE DOING THEIR JOB

If you see no obvious cracks or tears in the gasket (which is the piece of rubber that goes around the door of your refrigerator) but still suspect that it's not sealing properly, there are two ways to see if it needs replacement.

• Take a dollar bill and close the door on it. There should be a little resistance when you pull it out.

• Put a work light with a wattage of 100 to 150 inside the compartment. Close the door and look around the seal for light leaks. If you see light it's time to replace the gasket.

2) If the legs are adjusted with screws use your screwdriver to raise or lower them until the unit is sitting properly.

3) If the legs adjust by screwing, the fastest way to level the unit is to tilt it back and place the block of wood underneath to hold it up while you turn the leveler legs. (Counterclockwise will raise the unit, clockwise will lower it.) Make adjustments until it's level.

MAKE-IT-EASY PROJECT #10-8
Replacing a Refrigerator Door Gasket

A door gasket is easy to replace as long as you do it in steps. After you've replaced the gasket, a good maintenance idea is to rub the gasket with a little mineral oil. It'll keep the gasket flexible and make it less likely to crack. Replacing the gaskets on a dishwasher is a similar process.

Level: Beginner
Tools: Screwdriver or nut driver
Materials: Replacement gasket (exact)

1) Soak the replacement gasket in warm water to make it more flexible and easier to work with. Unplug the refrigerator.

2) Start at the top of the door and loosen (don't remove) the retaining screws or nuts. Slip the old gasket out and slide the new one in. Retighten the screws. Move to the side and repeat the process all around the door.

MAKE-IT-EASY PROJECT # 10-9
Sagging Doors

Eventually refrigerator doors will start to sag—it's just a gravity thing. When they do, they start to cost you money because the seal is compromised and cold air escapes, making the unit work harder to keep food cold.

Level: Beginner
Tools: Screwdriver or nut driver

1) Gently pry off the plastic cap with the screwdriver. Use the nut driver or screwdriver to tighten screws or nuts. Lift the door from the end as you tighten. If the freezer and refrigerator have separate doors, you'll have to remove the freezer door in order to get to the refrigerator door.

MAKE-IT-EASY PROJECT #10-10
STRAIGHTENING WARPED REFRIGERATOR DOORS

Refrigerator doors are plastic and they're easy to realign.

Level: Beginner
Tools: Screwdriver

1) Underneath the rubber gasket that seals the door are retaining screws. Loosen them slightly and twist the door until it's tight against the frame. Retighten the screws.

MAKE-IT-EASY PROJECT #10-11
Replacing a Faulty Refrigerator Switch

You should check the on/off switches that operate when the door opens and closes to make sure they're working. If you have two switches, one usually controls the light and the other turns on the fan in the freezer. A switch that stays on all the time costs you money because the refrigerator is working overtime. Open the door and push the light switch by hand. If the light doesn't go off, it needs to be replaced. On the other hand, if you push the fan switch and it doesn't turn on, it needs to be replaced as well.

Level: Beginner
Tools: Screwdriver * Continuity tester
Materials: Replacement switches (if necessary)

1) Unplug the refrigerator. The switches are removed by prying them gently from their mounting holes with a screwdriver. Disconnect the wires by pulling them off their connections.

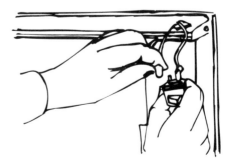

2) Test the switches with the continuity tester. On the light switch the tester should come on when the switch is out. On the fan switch the tester should light when the switch is pushed in.

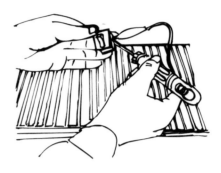

If the switch is faulty, get an exact replacement and reset the connections. If the switches are working properly, there's a wiring problem in the refrigerator itself and you need to call for a service check.

DRYERS AND WHAT AILS THEM

Dryers are mechanically quite simple. Mostly what they need is to be kept clean and free of lint—which accumulates everywhere. The first step is to clean the lint filter after every use. The second step is to clean the exhaust duct at least once a year. Use your trusty vacuum cleaner and also shake the duct to clean it out. While you've got the duct off, clean the vent to the outside with a coat hanger or other stiff piece of wire. It's very important that the duct doesn't have any low spots or sags—they'll fill up with the lint and eventually block the opening.

DRYERS, MOISTURE AND HEAT LOSS— *A SOLUTION*

Dryers fill the laundry room (and the rest of the house) with moist air as they pull the moisture out of the clothes. That's one of the reasons they need to vent to the out-side—otherwise you'll have serious condensation prob-lems. But vents, as you remember when we talked about insulation and weatherproofing, are a prime source of heat loss and are a great way for cold air to enter your home when you're not using the dryer. Electric dryers can be hooked into a return duct on your furnace (the bonus is that all that hot air goes into the general system), but gas dry-ers have to vent outside. If you're losing a lot of heat through the dryer vent during the winter months, you can fill a cloth bag with fiberglass insulation and put it in the dryer vent opening when you're not using the dryer.

REMEMBER THAT YOU HAVE TO REMOVE THE BAG WHEN YOU USE THE DRYER. Put a note up just in case you forget.

This may seem like a pain in the neck but if you live in a really cold climate it'll save you money.

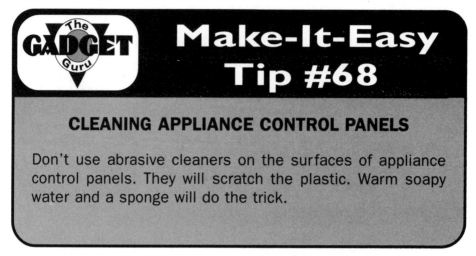

CLEANING APPLIANCE CONTROL PANELS

Don't use abrasive cleaners on the surfaces of appliance control panels. They will scratch the plastic. Warm soapy water and a sponge will do the trick.

It's a good idea to remove the front panel occasionally and vacuum around the inside.

MAKE-IT-EASY PROJECT #10-12
Replacing a Dryer's Door Seal

If the seal on your dryer door is hard, cracked and flaking, it's time to replace it. The seal should come from the supplier with a special heat-resistant silicone adhesive. If not you'll need some to glue it into place.

Level: Beginner
Tools: Putty knife
Materials: RTV silicone adhesive * Mineral spirits
Also: Cleaning rags

1) Remove the old seal and clean the ring well with mineral spirits.

2) Apply the silicone to the ring and press it into place with a putty knife.

MAKE-IT-EASY PROJECT #10-13
Replacing a Dryer Drum Belt

If the motor is running but the drum's not turning, the belt is probably broken or stretched. While it may seem like a big deal to take the front and top off the dryer, it's not—and the drum belt is easy to replace, sort of like threading a reel to reel tape recorder.

Level: Beginner
Tools: Putty knife wrapped in masking tape * Screwdriver or nut driver
Materials: Replacement drum belt * Replacement idler pulley (if necessary)

1) Unplug the dryer. If you have a gas dryer, follow the instructions for turning it off as well. Have a container handy to hold loose hardware.

2) Remove the toeplate by pressing in on the spring clips with your putty knife.

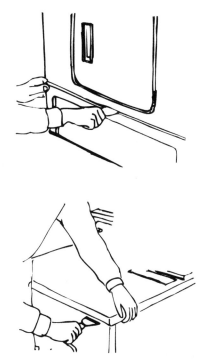

3) Remove the top lid by inserting your taped putty knife between the top and the front about two inches from the edge. Push the knife to release the spring clips. Lift it up and lean it against a wall or tie a piece of string to it so it won't fall backwards. On some models the screws for the lid are underneath the lip.

4) Remove the front panel by taking out the screws on the bottom and the top.

5) You'll see the drum belt wrapped around the drum. Underneath the drum of the dryer you'll find the idler pulley and the motor. Push the idler pulley to release tension on the belt. Remove the belt by sliding it off the drum.

6) If you find that the idler pulley is defective, remove it and replace it. It will either be hooked from a bracket, or be screw or clip mounted.

7) Slide the new belt onto the drum, aligning it along the marks left by the old one. Feed it through the idler pulley and around the motor pulley.

8) Reassemble the panels in the order you took them off. You're done.

Make-It-Easy Tip #69

DON'T PUSH YOUR VACUUM CLEANER AROUND— SOME EASY MAINTENANCE TIPS

Whether your vacuum cleaner is an upright or a canister it operates the same way. A fan driven by a motor draws the dirt and whatever else is on the floor up into a bag. Because vacuum cleaners are so simple mechanically most of the problems come from lack of maintenance—and not noticing that nail, bottle cap or quarter in time to stop it from being sucked up inside where it can do damage to the fan or become clogged in the hose.

- Always check the floor for large objects before you go to work. Shut the vacuum off immediately if something too big gets pulled inside. (You'll know because the vacuum cleaner will go nuts.) Don't restart the vacuum until you've cleared the object.
- As you do with other appliances, check the power cord and plug frequently for damage.
- Don't fill the bag beyond the manufacturer's recommended limit. It's clearly marked.
- If you have filters on the vacuum cleaner change them frequently. It saves wear and tear on the motor.
- There are vacuum cleaners designed specifically for liquids. Unless yours is made for the job don't use it to clean up spills.
- Clear a clogged hose with a broomstick or garden hose. Do it gently so you don't damage the vacuum cleaner hose in the process.
- Drive belts wear out and lose their tension, resulting in poor cleaning action. Follow the instructions in your manual; they're easy to replace.
- Clean the brushes frequently with a comb; they get clogged with hair, which affects their ability to lift the dirt from the surface. The bristles will also wear down in time and the roller should be replaced when they become short and stubby.
- Hair also gets caught in the groove that holds the drive belt in place and can make it slip. Cut the stuff away with a utility knife.

DEALING WITH DISHWASHERS

I think dishwashers have gotten a bad rap over the years. Many people consider them a luxury, but there are some interesting benefits to having one. First, they use less water than you would if you did the dishes by hand. Second, because of the high pressure and the temperature of the water when they're draining, they help keep all of the drain pipes in your home clear and free of clogs. Third, they're one of the major modern conveniences.

Dishwasher Troubleshooting

Use your manual's diagram as a guide to find solutions to the following problems.

DOESN'T FILL

• Sounds simple, but make sure the water is turned on.
• Check the float and see if anything is clogging the opening.
• Check the inlet screen valve and see if it's clogged.

DOESN'T DRAIN

• See if the drain filter, strainer, pump or drain valve is clogged. Make sure the drain hose isn't looped or kinked.

DOESN'T CLEAN

• Use a meat thermometer to make sure the water is hot enough (130 to 140 degrees). Hold it under the hot water faucet to get a reading.
• Again, check for clogs and make sure the detergent dispenser is not gummed up, which prevents it from releasing soap. Dishwashing detergent also tends to get hard and lumpy when it gets old. It's not necessarily a savings to buy it in quantity.

CHANGING HOSES

If hoses are cracked and hard they need to be replaced. Buy exact replacements and save the worn ones so you can use them as a model to cut the new ones to the proper length with a mat knife. Most hoses are attached to appliances with spring clips. Put on a pair of safety goggles and get your pliers. Squeeze the prongs of the clip with the pliers and slide it off the coupling. Remove the hose and replace it. If the hose is stuck, slit it with a utility knife and peel it away.

LEAKS

- Check the gasket on the dishwasher door to be sure it's in good shape.
- Look for clogs in the inlet and outlet valves, check that the seal on the pump is good, and make sure the clamps on the hoses are tight.

OIL AND WATER DON'T MIX—
PREVENTING LEAKS AND PUMP FAILURES
IN YOUR DISHWASHER

After the dishwasher's cycle, a certain amount of water remains in the bottom. Why? To keep the seals and O-rings moist and therefore protect the seal. If the water evaporates, the seals dry up, the pump could freeze and leaks will follow. If you're not using the dishwasher for an extended period, pour a little mineral oil in the bottom. The oil will float on top of the water and prevent it from evaporating.

PART FOUR

Creating a Household Safety Routine— Preparing for and Dealing with Emergencies

Throughout this book I've talked a lot about safety when you're working on projects and how good old common sense and following the rules will protect you from injury. It's all about routine, getting used to doing things in a logical and thoughtful order so you can know what to expect when you confront problems and, more importantly, preventing things from becoming problems. Now we're going to talk about what to do when things go wrong.

I think a lot of us avoid making preparations for emergencies simply because it's an unpleasant job. Putting fire extinguishers and smoke detectors around the house, for instance, is a reminder that fire can strike anytime, no matter how safe we feel. But I know that being as prepared as possible to deal with the unexpected has actually given me peace of mind. It's comforting to know that I'm ready to take charge in a time of crisis, that I can take care of my family.

In the same sense, knowing what to do when a pipe bursts, a washing machine overflows, or an electrical problem occurs, reminds us we're in charge and that we have some control over unexpected events. I think that developing a common sense household safety and emergency routine is one of the most important things we can do for ourselves and those we love.

CHAPTER ELEVEN

When Things Go Wrong—Handling Emergencies in the Home

FIRE

Fire can strike in even the most carefully maintained and cared for home. You should install smoke detectors on every level according to the recommendations of the local fire codes and manufacturers. Stock the house with fire extinguishers and learn how to use them. (We'll get to that in a minute.) Have flash-lights near every bed and keep them supplied with fresh batteries or install the rechargeable type in convenient outlets. Some emergency rechargeable flash-lights attach to an outlet standing by for a power outage. When the power does cut off, the flashlight automatically illuminates, making it simple to locate.

SMOKE DETECTOR

COMMON SENSE STEPS TO PREVENT FIRES

Follow the basic rules of fire safety:

1) Store flammable liquids in closed containers away from sources of heat.

2) Store oily rags in closed metal containers (so they won't combust spontaneously). Dispose of them as hazardous waste as soon as possible.

3) Don't fill tanks of gas powered tools while the engine is running or hot.

4) Keep all stove vents free of grease. Clean them regularly.

5) Never leave anything unattended on the stove and keep pot handles turned inward so you won't knock them accidentally.

6) Don't let curtains fall into or against electric heating elements.

7) Make sure light bulbs are not touching lampshades.

8) Don't let children play with matches or use appliances unattended.

9) Keep all appliances, big and small, clean and free of debris and in good working order.

10) Always use a fire screen when you're using your fireplace.

11) Have your chimney cleaned once a year.

12) Don't overload electrical circuits and use only properly rated fuses.

13) Don't allow rubbish to pile up in corners of the basement or garage.

BE PREPARED—MAKE AN ESCAPE PLAN

Here's what the people at First Alert tell us to prepare for, and act on, if there's a fire in our home.

1) Never ignore the smoke detector—better a false alarm than a tragedy.

2) Discuss and rehearse an escape plan with the entire family. Make sure everyone knows at least two exits from each room.

3) Always feel a door or doorknob before you open the door. If either is hot, use another route.

4) Crawl on the floor. Smoke and heat rise so there'll be less heat and smoke the lower you are to the ground.

5) Meet at a prearranged spot outside your house so you can know for sure that everyone is safe.

6) Call the fire department after you get outside. Borrow a neighbor's phone.

7) Never go back inside a burning building. Once you're out, stay out. It's the fire department's job to put out the fire and perform emergency rescues.

FIRE EXTINGUISHERS CAN SAVE YOUR LIFE AND YOUR HOME

You should have working and properly maintained ABC-type fire extinguishers in the kitchen, basement, garage, utility room and anyplace else the possibility of fire exists. They should be hung on their brackets and placed near doorways on unblocked areas of the wall. Everyone in your family who is capable of understanding how to use them should know where they are.

But, what's important to understand here is that no one should ever be a hero. You can prepare yourself to handle small fires effectively, but if at any moment things seem to be getting out of control, leave the house and call the fire department. Staying is not worth the risk.

Here's what you need to know about fire extinguishers, how to operate them and how to use them on common small fires.

Fire extinguishers are rated in classes by the kinds of fires they deal with.

• **Class A** Designed for wood, paper, rubber and many plastics.

• **Class B** Designed for oil, solvents, grease, gasoline, kerosene and other flammable liquids. Class B extinguishers are filled with dry chemicals.

• **Class C** Designed for electrical fires. Class C extinguishers are also filled with dry chemicals.

The people who make fire extinguishers have also come up with a so-called multi-purpose type, or ABC, which can be used to fight most small fires in the home. I recommend the ABC type because if there's an emergency you don't have to think about which extinguisher to grab.

You're looking for a fire extinguisher in the 2½ to 7 pound range. It's extremely important that you follow the manufacturer's recommendations for longevity of the unit and read the pressure gauge to make sure it's within the recommended range. These things are no good if they don't work.

Read the instructions carefully so that you know how to use a fire extinguisher before the need arises. They all operate in essentially the same way. First, be sure that the fire isn't between you and an exit in case you have to leave in a hurry. Pull the pin or other release mechanism.

AIM AT THE BASE OF THE FIRE AND SWEEP FROM SIDE TO SIDE UNTIL THE FIRE IS OUT.

Stand about 6 to 10 feet away from the fire and near an exit. Pull the release mechanism and spray in a side to side motion at the base of the flames. The fire may seem to grow before it starts to go out. If flames get scattered by the spray move back and extinguish them as well. Keep spraying until the fire is out and then watch carefully to make sure it doesn't *flashback*, or start again.

IF THE FIRE IS ELECTRICAL SHUT OFF THE MAIN SERVICE PANEL AFTER YOU'VE EXTINGUISHED THE FIRE AND CALL THE FIRE DEPARTMENT.

How to Put Out a Fire in a Pan

1) Don't move the pan.

2) Turn off the burners and the fan in the range hood if it's on.

3) Put on an oven mitt or protect your hand with a hot pad. Slide the lid of the pan or use a platter that is larger than the diameter of the pan over it to smother the flames. It's important to slide the covering over the fire, because if you pop it on top the flames may spread. If the flames persist pour baking soda on the fire. Once it's out let the pan cool before removing it from the stove.

How to Put Out a Fire on the Stove Top

If the fire has spread from the pot to the stove top, do the following. As before, don't move the pan or pot.

1) Turn off the burners and the range fan.

2) Pour baking soda generously on the fire until it's extinguished. If baking soda doesn't do the job use a fire extinguisher.

IMPORTANT: NEVER PUT WATER, FLOUR OR BAKING *POWDER* ON A STOVE TOP FIRE—IT WILL ONLY SPREAD THE FLAMES.

How to Put Out a Fire in the Oven

If you have a fire in the oven, it can sometimes be put out by closing the oven door and turning off the oven. This shuts off the supply of oxygen. If that doesn't work, you'll have to go to the fire extinguisher.

ELECTRICAL SAFETY

Preparation and a good maintenance program are the keys to staying ahead of electrical emergencies. Supply your home with candles, matches, flashlights, extra batteries and a camping lantern. Keep them in an accessible place and make sure everyone in the family knows where they are.

IMPORTANT: IF YOU HAVE A POWER OUTAGE, YOU CAN PROTECT YOUR APPLIANCES FROM THE POWER SURGE THAT WILL COME WHEN POWER IS RESTORED BY TURNING OFF OR UNPLUGGING THEM.

1) Take your family on a tour of the house and show them the main service panel. Explain how the circuit breakers and the main disconnect work, and show them the circuit map you prepared so they can turn off service if there's a problem.

I suggest keeping a rubber mat on the floor in front of the service panel so that people are protected in case the floor is damp.

IN AN EMERGENCY, WEAR A PAIR OF RUBBER GLOVES TO SHUT OFF THE POWER, OR USE A WOODEN STICK OR BROOM HANDLE TO FLIP THE SWITCH. PROTECT YOURSELF FROM BECOMING A CONDUCTOR BY USING ONLY ONE HAND.

2) Buy and use electrical appliances and fixtures that carry the Underwriter's Laboratory seal of approval.

3) Read and keep all manuals and information that come with electrical appliances and power tools.

4) If you notice an odor or see smoke from an electrical outlet or appliance, use a rubber glove or heavy towel to protect your hand and unplug the appliance. Flip the circuit breaker immediately. Try to identify the problem and call in a professional if necessary. Don't use the appliance again until it's been fixed.

5) Keep all electrical equipment and appliances maintained and in good repair. Check for frayed cords and damaged plugs, and don't overload circuits.

6) Always unplug any appliance and shut down the power at the service panel before you attempt any repair.

WATER AND ELECTRICITY ARE A POTENTIALLY FATAL COMBINATION. DO NOT TOUCH SWITCHES, OUTLETS, SOCKETS OR CORDS IF YOUR HANDS AND FEET ARE WET OR YOU ARE STANDING ON A DAMP FLOOR. DON'T TOUCH FAUCETS OR PIPES WHILE YOU ARE HANDLING ANYTHING ELECTRICAL.

SHUTTING OFF A SPARKING OR SMOKING SWITCH

Stand away from the switch and shut it off with a stick or wooden spoon. Shut off power at the main service panel and call the electrician to replace the switch and check out the system before you restore power.

Dealing with Shock—FREEING SOMEONE FROM ELECTRICAL CURRENT

Knock on wood it'll never happen, but if someone touches live current he or she will be in danger. Most often the shock will throw the person away from the contact, but sometimes the muscles will freeze or the person will be caught and held in place.

Unplug the appliance, or shut off the power at the service panel. If that isn't possible use a wooden broom handle or a wooden chair and knock the person away. You must break the contact.

IMPORTANT: COVER ALL OUTLETS WITH CHILD–PROOF CAPS TO PREVENT CHILDREN FROM POKING AND PLAYING WITH THEM.

EMERGENCY TREATMENT FOR SHOCK VICTIMS

Call 911 for assistance immediately. Be concise and clear when you answer the questions asked. If the victim is breathing and there are no head or neck injuries place him or her in what First Aid instructors call the *recovery position*. Tilt the head back with the face to one side and the tongue forward to open the air passage. Remain calm and keep the victim comfortable until help arrives.

WATER AND PLUMBING

Most plumbing emergencies involve burst or leaking pipes. Leaks can occur for any number of reasons. Good maintenance can prevent many leaks. If you notice leaks from fixtures or appliances, shut off the nearest supply valve and assess the damage in order to make repairs.

Burst pipes most often occur when water freezes in the pipes and expands. If you lose general power during the winter or your furnace goes off for any period of time, there is a danger of pipes freezing.

• If you find a pipe that is beginning to freeze (you can tell by reduced water flow through a faucet and also by feeling for cold spots on a pipe), go around your house and turn on the faucets so that a trickle of water is flowing through them (running water won't freeze). Because they're usually buried beneath the frost line, drain lines are unlikely to freeze but if you notice that water is backing up, call a plumber to check the drain lines.

• Turn off the supply valves to your toilet and drain the tank and bowl by flushing.

• If a pipe is frozen but not burst (typically there will be no flow through the faucet), turn on the nearest faucet and turn down the main valve about ¼ to lower water pressure. Use your hair dryer to thaw the pipe. Starting with the faucet, hold the dryer 3 to 4 inches away and move up the pipe to the source. (You can tell where the freeze is by touch: it will definitely be colder. You might also see a bulge.) When water begins to flow from the faucet, restore the main valve to full open. The additional pressure will help break the ice.

• If the pipe is damaged, have it replaced. Insulate all exposed pipes with electric heating tape or foam insulating tubes as soon as possible.

What You Can Do until the Plumber Arrives— EMERGENCY REPAIRS FOR BROKEN OR BURST PIPES

1) If the leak in the pipe is very small, try filling it with a toothpick or pencil lead and wrapping it tightly with electrical tape.

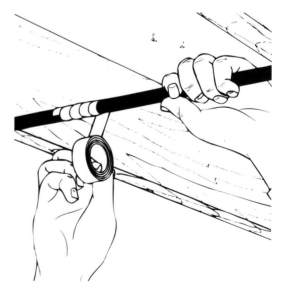

2) Another solution to small leaks is plumber's epoxy. This adhesive makes almost as permanent a bond as the pipe itself. The epoxy comes in two tubes and needs to be mixed. Follow the directions for cleaning and prepping the pipe. Use rubber gloves to apply.

3) Temporary repairs can be made for larger leaks in a couple of different ways.

• Go to the hardware or plumbing supply, and get a length of rubber tubing the same size as the pipe and two hose clamps. Measure a piece of tubing that is longer than the hole. Slit it with a mat knife and wrap it around the pipe. Attach the hose clamps with a screwdriver. Check for leaks. An alternative is a piece of inner tube wrapped tightly around the leak and attached with hose clamps.

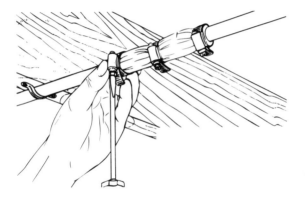

• Plumbing supply shops carry an item called a pipe leak clamp. It's a hinged collar that comes with a piece of rubber. Place the rubber over the leak, wrap the collar around the rubber sleeve and tighten the nuts. This works very well and will get you by until the pipe can be replaced.

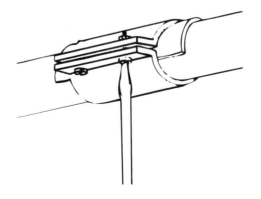

GETTING RID OF WATER BUILDUP IN A CEILING

If a tub or toilet overflows upstairs or if a slow leak has built up over time, water will build up in the plaster or drywall in the ceiling below. The ceiling material will act like a sponge and hold the water until the ceiling begins to sag with the weight. Eventually it will burst. You can do some damage control with a nail or your carpenter's awl and a bucket. Use the nail to puncture at the center of the sag and the bucket to collect the water. It's messy but less messy than waiting until it bursts of its own accord.

After you've drained the ceiling make an appointment with a professional to repair the cause of the leak and replace the damaged section.

After the Flood — CLEANING UP WATER IN THE BASEMENT

If the worst happens, a major pipe bursts for instance, and you find you've got two or three feet of standing water in the basement, make an appointment with your plumber. Then go to the tool rental outlet and get a sump pump. A sump pump is a suction pump to which you attach a length of garden hose to drain water out of the house. Sump pumps are operated either by gasoline or electricity (electric sump pumps are the easiest to deal with). You'll save time on the plumber's labor bill by draining the basement yourself.

Get instructions and advice on operation from the rental house. Generally, the pump must be lowered into the water before turning it on, otherwise you could burn out the motor.

Make sure you are wearing rubber boots and that you are well away from the water when you plug in the pump. Standing on the basement stairs is a good idea. From this point on it's a matter of patience; you stand there, hold the pump and wait for it to do its thing.

When the pump is no longer sucking water (usually when the level is less than ½ inch) get your mops and bucket and sop up the remainder.

GAS AND CARBON MONOXIDE

GAS—In its natural state the gas we use to run our appliances is odorless and colorless; you'd never know it was there until it was too late. The odor we smell is added by the utility company to let us know there's a problem.

• If you smell gas in a room, shut off any flame and open windows to clear the fumes. Don't touch switches or unplug appliances from outlets—a spark could set off an explosion. Once the room is clear, consult the appliance's manual for information on relighting pilot lights if any are out.

• If the odor remains or if you come home and smell gas, gather your family and **LEAVE THE HOUSE IMMEDIATELY**. Call the utility company from a neighbor's phone and don't go back inside until the problem is fixed.

SHUTTING OFF THE GAS SUPPLY TO AN APPLIANCE

The valve that controls the flow of gas to your stove or water heater works on the same principle as a plumbing supply valve. It should be located nearby on the pipe that feeds the appliance. Turn the handle perpendicular to the gas pipe to shut off the gas.

The main gas valve will be located at the gas meter. Keep a pair of channel locks nearby to turn the handle perpendicular to the main gas pipe.

CARBON MONOXIDE—The fumes that come from any combustible source (wood, gas, kerosene and the like) contain carbon monoxide. Breathing carbon monoxide for an extended length of time can cause serious illness and even death. It's extremely important to vent everything properly and keep all vents and ducts clean and free of debris. Have your chimney and heating system inspected yearly. Companies like First Alert make carbon monoxide detectors that sense its presence the same way smoke detectors sense smoke.

IMPORTANT: DON'T RUN YOUR CAR IN A CLOSED GARAGE AND ALWAYS START POWER MOWERS AND OTHER GASO-LINE POWERED APPLIANCES OUTSIDE.

IMPORTANT: INSIDE YOUR HOME NEVER USE CHAR-COAL, PROPANE OR WOOD BURNING GRILLS INTENDED FOR USE OUTDOORS. THERE IS NO VENTING FOR THE FUMES AND YOU ARE VULNERABLE TO CARBON MONOXIDE POISONING.

PART FIVE

Hiring a Professional Contractor— Without Losing Your Mind

There are many reasons to become a household guru, and we've talked about a lot them throughout the course of this book: saving money, the satisfaction that comes from taking care of business on your own and the confidence that comes from knowing how things work, to name a few. But there are also a lot of reasons to hire somebody to handle projects for you. Some jobs are just beyond our range of skills, and even if they were something we could handle, sometimes we just don't have the time to tackle them. When you're considering a costly addition to your home, for example, you want the best work possible.

After all, you're making an investment that will hopefully add to the value of your home and improve the quality of your family's life. You want to bring in a pro to do the job and you want to hire one who'll do it right the first time and at the price you're ready to pay.

In the following chapter we'll talk about how to find and work with a professional contractor. But I'd like to note that you can also use this common sense information to seek out good, hard working professionals such as plumbers, electricians, carpenters and other craftsmen to do smaller and less complicated projects around your home.

CHAPTER TWELVE

It's a Jungle Out There— How to Find, Hire and Work with a Professional Contractor or a Competent Tradesman

If you're about to spend a big chunk of your hard earned money or take out a high-priced loan to do some work on your home, you've got to be sure you're going to get what you want. It may be the second biggest investment you're going to make (the first was buying the home itself) and you need somebody you can trust to do the work. The problem is that most homeowners don't have any idea what's involved in a renovation and they sure don't know what a contractor actually does.

The renovation business is full of contractors ranging from top notch to those you may consider downright thieves who'll take your money and run, to incompetents who have the gift of making you believe they're old world craftsmen while they're in the process of ruining your home.

The contractors you want to learn to spot and avoid are those who disappear right after you give them the first payment. Those who try to jack up the price halfway through the job, who won't return your calls and are never on the job site. Those who suddenly can't be found when the deck starts to sag, or promise endlessly to take care of the leak in the basement but never deliver.

These people are the bad news in home renovation and construction.

FINDING THE RIGHT PERSON FOR THE JOB

A good friend of mine who is an architect in the Northeast and has spent a lot of time dealing with contractors told me that working with a good contractor is a little like using the right tool for the right job. A good, honest contractor makes your life easy while a bad one makes it a living hell. But according to my friend, the good news is that responsible, talented and honest contractors, the kind who have sawdust in their veins and love their work, do exist.

You just have to know how to find them.

My friend broke contractors down into three separate but not equal categories. He called them the pros, the crooks and everybody else.

1) The **PROS** are the ones who will get your job done right. They are proud of what they do and it's their business to make you satisfied. They are trustworthy, talented and honest. They're real **GENERAL CONTRACTORS** in the best sense. That means they can handle a lot of different projects successfully, partially because they know what they do well and also know people who can do what they can't. They know that their reputation and livelihood depend upon making you happy. Other than delivering a top notch job on time, they strive to be able to use you as a future recommendation. My friend told me when I found the contractor of my dreams to chain him (or her) in the basement so I'd always know where he (or she) was.

2) The **CROOKS** could care less about the quality of their work or their reputation. Their primary interest is doing as much renovation on your bank account as possible and being gone before you realize what's happening. It's safe to say they don't have your best interests at heart.

3) **EVERYBODY ELSE** is the largest category because contractors are just like the rest of the human race—most are basically honest, skilled in certain areas, likely to exaggerate their abilities and apt to take a little advantage if the opportunity presents itself. For the most part they're well-intentioned and they probably do some things well. If you know what these things are, you might get what you want. They might do a good job or not, depending on the circumstances and their abilities.

G A **DGET** The Guru

Make It Easy
Tip #72

PRICE, TIME, SCALE AND QUALITY—
YOU CAN'T HAVE YOUR CAKE AND EAT IT TOO

My architect friend points out that it's just a fact of life in the construction business—you can't have the biggest house for the lowest price, built in the shortest time, of the highest quality. The variables of **Price, Time, Scale** and **Quality** are how you begin to make decisions about how you will approach your renovation. You need to figure the variables into the job, and one or more of them will usually be fixed (inflexible).

The formula is pretty simple. For instance, if you have a limited budget, then the scope of your project will be smaller, time will be a factor, and you probably will not be able to afford the very best. Or, if it's June 30th and the project needs to be finished before school starts in September, then you can figure the price will be higher, and perhaps the quality a bit lower (good finish work takes time), or the scale of your project will need to be down scaled.

The first thing to do is decide how the variables affect you.

If **PRICE** is your primary concern, you know you'll have to make compromises on scope and quality.

If **TIME** is your concern, you can expect to pay a higher price, especially if you want to maintain high quality, or, more likely, you'll have to lower your expectations. On the other hand, if time pressure doesn't factor in, you can often save money by proceeding at a slower pace and still get quality work.

If **SCALE** is the central issue (you need the addition and it has to be a certain size), you'll compromise either price or quality or both.

If **QUALITY** is at the heart of the matter, you'll have to spend the time and money necessary to get exactly what you want. And, you'll be happy to do it.

STARTING THE SEARCH

One of the biggest traps homeowners fall into as they start seeking a contractor is pretending to know more than they do about the project. It's human nature not to want to appear naive. This attitude can make us easy marks for the crooks because the more you pretend to know the more they can take advantage. So, when a crook tells us the roof needs to be replaced because the *whatchamacallit* is cracked we might pretend to know what he is talking about, grimace, and tell him to do what needs to be done rather than do a little homework and get the facts.

If you've spent the time using my book to get to know your home and how it works, you've got a real advantage in dealing with contractors because you'll be far less likely to fall for exaggerated and dishonest claims, phony estimates and unnecessary repairs.

RENOVATION BY THE NUMBERS

1) KNOW WHAT YOU'RE DOING AND WHY

In order to start planning a project you need to consider a couple of things.

How long do you plan to stay in the place you're going to work on?

Unless the renovation adds real equity to your home it may not be smart to spend a lot of money if you're intending to be out the door a year after you're finished.

Will the result be worth the expense?

You need to think about whether or not you're really going to want a combination Ping-Pong room and sauna in five years.

2) HAVE A PLAN IN PLACE

You need a well-considered plan before you start looking for a contractor. There are lots of options these days. You can hire an architect or a designer, buy a standard blueprint, download information from the internet or make sketches on a piece of paper yourself.

Do your research, look for things you like in friends' homes, pore over magazines, watch all the home shows on cable for ideas. Once you have an idea of what you want, learn as much as you can about what's going to be required to get the job done. That'll give you a real edge when you start interviewing contractors.

3) ASK QUESTIONS

The first rule is—stay away from the yellow pages and television ads. It's not that honest contractors don't advertise, it's just that the real pros get most of their jobs by referral, not from the telephone book.

The best way to learn about a contractor's credentials and reputation is the way we learn about anything else—ask questions of people who know. The best sources are homeowners and architects that the contractor has worked for. An honest contractor should be more than happy to provide a client list—if he isn't, that's a good clue that he may not be the one for you.

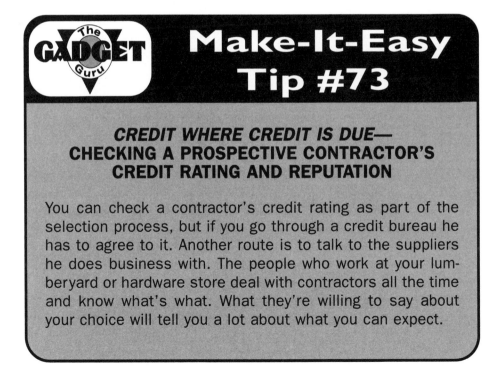

The Gadget Guru Make-It-Easy Tip #73

CREDIT WHERE CREDIT IS DUE— CHECKING A PROSPECTIVE CONTRACTOR'S CREDIT RATING AND REPUTATION

You can check a contractor's credit rating as part of the selection process, but if you go through a credit bureau he has to agree to it. Another route is to talk to the suppliers he does business with. The people who work at your lumberyard or hardware store deal with contractors all the time and know what's what. What they're willing to say about your choice will tell you a lot about what you can expect.

CONSUMER PROTECTION—
CHECK YOUR CONTRACTOR'S LICENSE

Many areas of the country require contractors to be licensed by the state. Find out if this is the case in your area—if it is make sure your contractor is licensed and in good standing. Don't work with an unlicensed contractor where licenses are required—there's probably a good reason why he doesn't have one and it isn't worth the risk.

Look for homeowners who've completed projects similar to what you want to do. The guy may have done a great job on someone's garage but if you're doing something that requires good solid interior finish work you may not find a fit.

Here are a few questions to ask.

• *Was the homeowner not only satisfied but really happy with the job?*

• *If there was an architect on the job, was he satisfied with the quality of the work and the relationship with the contractor?*

• *Did the homeowner like him and his employees? Were they neat and orderly as they worked?*

• *How accurate and complete was his budget? Did he provide alternatives that made a difference in price but didn't compromise the scale of the job? Did he stick with his price as the job progressed? Of course, there are always unforeseen and unexpected problems that can change the nature of a job but they should be obvious and clearly reasonable.*

• *Was the contractor easy to deal with and on time? Did he answer questions clearly, and was he available for meetings?*

• *Was he organized? Did he keep track of quality control on the job and make sure the workers met his (and your) standards?*

• *Did he keep the homeowner appraised of the progress of the job and warn of problems so there was ample time to come up with alternative solutions?*

• *Have there been problems since the work was completed and was the contractor willing to resolve them?*

• *Would the homeowner use the contractor again and recommend him to friends?*

4) INTERVIEWING PROSPECTIVE CONTRACTORS

Arrange to meet the contractors who are possibilities. Don't hide the fact that you're shopping around. Talk to them about what you want to do and see what they've done that's similar to it. If they offer to show you jobs in progress, set up meetings with former clients, and take you to homes they've worked on, consider it a good sign that they're on the level.

5) GETTING QUOTES

Narrow the list after the first interview, go over what you want and ask them to submit quotes, which are detailed written bids. The quote should include materials, pricing breakdowns and a building schedule with a defined completion date. Without being rude make them aware that there's some competition. You'll get their best price. Ask questions and expect clear answers. If they can't be clear discussing your project with you at the kitchen table, they won't be able to once the job is in progress either.

6) COMPARE THE BIDS

One sign of a good contractor is how fast he gets back to you. Unless what you're doing is pretty simple, it shouldn't be the next day, but it shouldn't take a month either. Look over the bids and see how they compare. They should all be in the same range and you should notice that they have similarities in how they will approach the work. Be careful of bids that are too low and too high.

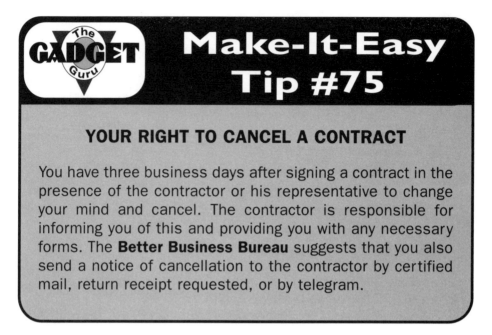

YOUR RIGHT TO CANCEL A CONTRACT

You have three business days after signing a contract in the presence of the contractor or his representative to change your mind and cancel. The contractor is responsible for informing you of this and providing you with any necessary forms. The **Better Business Bureau** suggests that you also send a notice of cancellation to the contractor by certified mail, return receipt requested, or by telegram.

7) MAKING THE FINAL CHOICE

Choosing your contractor is a combination of research and instinct. If the price is right you're going to have to decide about the intangibles. Can you work with him? Will you feel comfortable having his crew in your home during the construction? Does he seem like he really wants the job? Take your time—choosing the contractor is the most important renovation decision you're going to make. **DON'T EVER SUCCUMB TO HIGH PRESSURE SALES PITCHES.** Again, take your time—it's your home and your money.

BY THE NUMBERS—GOING TO WORK

1) MAKING THE BATTLE PLAN

Sit down with your choice and go over everything in detail. It's easy to make alterations on paper, it's expensive once the job is under way. Make sure the final plans are understood by both parties, and materials and equipment lists are complete. Common misunderstandings between contractors and clients center around what materials and supplies are to be provided by the contractor as part of the bid and what the client is expected to provide. You don't want any surprises on the job and neither does the contractor.

2) The Final Contract

The final contract between you and your contractor should include four categories—price, payment schedule, scope of work and schedule for completion. It should also be understood who's responsible for arranging building permits and code inspections. It is in your best interests to have your lawyer help you negotiate the contract to make sure you are protected in case of default by the contractor.

Price. Agree on a price that includes everything necessary to do the job and make sure the contractor understands that it's written in stone. Do be aware, however, that sometimes there are circumstances which can surprise everybody and be prepared to be fair and reasonable about the unexpected.

Payment Schedule. Don't ever pay all or even half the money on signing. Depending on the scale of the job the payment schedule may be broken into any number of payments based on completion of phases.

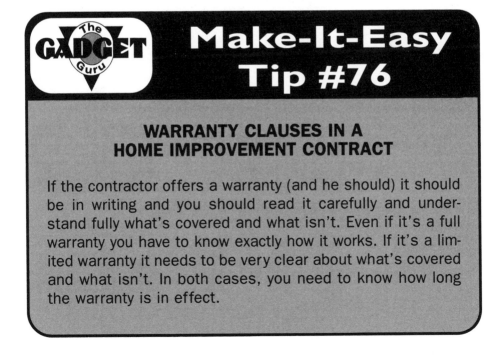

Make-It-Easy Tip #76

WARRANTY CLAUSES IN A HOME IMPROVEMENT CONTRACT

If the contractor offers a warranty (and he should) it should be in writing and you should read it carefully and understand fully what's covered and what isn't. Even if it's a full warranty you have to know exactly how it works. If it's a limited warranty it needs to be very clear about what's covered and what isn't. In both cases, you need to know how long the warranty is in effect.

Phases are points in the construction when specific work should be completed—such as rough construction, installation of plumbing and electrical, etc. The most common payment schedules for home renovation are based on three or four payments.

Make-It-Easy Tip #77

WHAT YOU NEED TO KNOW ABOUT LIEN LAWS

Lien laws are on the books in every state in the union. They're there to protect suppliers and other involved parties from financial loss in case someone like a contractor defaults on payments. The reason you need to know this is that the injured parties have one major recourse to recoup their losses—they go after you and your home.

The disastrous effect that liens can have on you and your family are enough reason alone to check out your contractor very carefully and stay on top of the job while it's in progress to make sure payments are being made as required.

If a contractor bails out on a job, the subcontractors and suppliers have usually between 60 and 90 days to file a lien on your property for payment and in most cases they will collect even if it means foreclosure.

In some states parties are required to notify you if they're filing a lien; in some states they can do it without your knowledge. I think it's very important that you understand the lien laws in your state and how they affect you. Check with an attorney who's knowledgeable in this area.

In some places subcontractors will file a lien on the property that will stay in effect until the work is finished. This is just a formality and is done to guarantee that the homeowner won't sell the property while the job is in progress. In this case you have to make sure that you all sign release of lien forms when work is completed.

While a three payment schedule is the most common, you might be able to find a contractor who will work on four, and it's to your advantage to try to negotiate the latter. The reason?

Usually the contractor's biggest outlay of money is in the beginning of the job—he has to buy materials. That's why he will often tell you he needs a large payment up front. If you can verify that your money is going directly to a supplier to pay for materials, that's fine, but here's the problem. Most often the contractor will actually buy from the supplier on credit. He'll use your money for something else. Now there's nothing wrong with this unless he skips town or doesn't finish the job. And if he's dumped a load of lumber purchased on credit on your lawn and he can't be found, the supplier will come after you and very likely put a lien on your property to pay the bill. (See Make-It-Easy Tip #77—What You Need To Know about Lien Laws.) You could end up in a situation where you've paid the contractor and now you have to pay the supplier as well.

The bottom line is don't pay any more up front than you absolutely have to, and if he says he's going to use it to buy materials, ask for proof.

WORKING OUT A THREE PAYMENT SCHEDULE

We'll take a look at a three payment schedule as an example for how to set one up.

The first payment should be made on signing the contract. It should be no more than a third of the total budget and preferably less.

The second payment should made be at about the halfway point based on the work schedule, but it should be a mutually agreed on and specific date. It should also be at a point before walls are sealed so you can check the electrical and plumbing work to be sure everything is up to standard and code. It's also the last time you'll really be able to make changes without a huge additional expense or to call him on things he should have done.

REMEMBER: The rule of thumb is that the contractor pays for his mistakes and you pay for yours.

The third payment should be scheduled on completion of the job. In the best of all possible worlds you should hold a portion of the final payment until things have settled down and you've had a chance to see that everything's just as you want it. Don't forget, you have to live there long after the contractor's swinging his hammer someplace else.

MAKE A PUNCH LIST AND KEEP TRACK OF IT

As the work nears completion, you and the contractor need to agree on what's left to be done. The agreement is called a punch list. It contains everything necessary to complete the entire job. The most important task you'll have as the job finishes is to keep track of what's left to do. No matter how good and honest the contractor is, he's a busy man, and once he's gone, it's hard to get him back. Make sure every item is checked off before you write the final check.

Scope of Work. You and the contractor must agree on everything necessary to complete the job, including quality of materials, level of work and completion dates. Know who's actually doing the work. It's common for the contractor to hire subcontractors for things like electrical and plumbing. You need to know who's responsible if a subcontractor's work is unacceptable.

Schedule for Completion. Agree on a work schedule, including a final completion date that, ideally, is on a specific date. It should be written in the contract. Break it down into phases as we discussed previously. Phases not only give you an idea of how the job is progressing but also give you a chance to keep track of whether or not you're on schedule and up to code.

REMEMBER: A good contractor wants to do a good job for you; not only would he like your business next time but he also wants your referral. Don't settle for anything less than you expect and make sure you're getting the best job for your renovation dollar.

MAKE THE MOST OF YOUR RENOVATION DOLLAR—WORK AND RESEARCH YOU CAN DO YOURSELF TO SAVE MONEY

Of course, you'll save a lot of money if you do all your own contracting, but it's a difficult and labor intensive undertaking, and you need to know what you're doing or you'll get burned. Still, there are several ways even a beginner can make a renovation budget go a little farther.

- Do any of the manual labor you can yourself. This includes demolition, basic painting, general insulation, and cleaning the construction site. You'll save money on wages to unskilled labor and have a good excuse to keep track of the job's progress.
- Spend a lot of time deciding what you want before you start the job. Be comfortable with your choices and stick with them. Changes are very expensive in midconstruction.
- Don't be tempted to go over your budget. It's easy in the heat of battle to give in and spend more than you wanted to. If something comes in at a higher price than you expected, cut back on something else. You'll enjoy the results a whole lot more if you're not worried about the extra money you had to spend.
- Research companies that supply materials and fixtures. Their 800 numbers are easy to find, and the sales people are generally helpful. Sometimes you can buy at a direct discount, and often you can buy at a reduced price seconds that have only minor flaws.

Make-It-Easy Tip #80

MAKING USE OF THE BBB—THE BETTER BUSINESS BUREAU IS YOUR FRIEND

The Better Business Bureau is a non-profit organization that exists to promote fair, honest and ethical business practices. They're a great resource for information on how a company has done business in the past. They collect and keep information that's available to consumers to help them make informed decisions about who to do business with.

They develop programs to encourage businesses to regulate and control their advertising and selling practices, and they will serve as a neutral third party to help settle disputes. They can give you information on how to contact your state office of Consumer Protection.

Check with your local bureau for more information or contact: The Council of Better Business Bureaus, 4200 Wilson Boulevard, Arlington, VA 22203 (703-276-0100).

HOW NOT TO GET RIPPED OFF IN AN EMERGENCY—BE PREPARED

When something big goes wrong in your home, you're in a very vulnerable position. You need something done and you need it done in a hurry. There's no time to check a plumber's credentials carefully when water is inching up the basement walls or have an extended conversation with a series of electricians while everything in your freezer is thawing out because of a failure in your electrical system.

In cases like these the Yellow Pages will certainly not be your friend. Many of the people who list themselves there are just waiting for calls like yours—emergencies mean higher charges and more money in their pockets. And they may take advantage of the crisis to bill you for work that doesn't need to be done. The only way to be sure you'll be dealt with fairly in an emergency is to have done your homework and compiled a list of honest plumbers, electricians and carpenters. Again, your local hardware people as well as friends and neighbors are great sources of information about the good guys.

It's also a good idea to have several names on your emergency list. Good craftsmen are usually busy, and it gives you better odds of finding someone quickly. I also suggest you use some of the people on general repair and maintenance projects so you can get to know them in non-emergency situations. Like all of us, craftsmen are more likely to rush to the aid of people they know than people they don't.

Also be aware that in some cases, even the good guys might charge you a higher rate for emergency work, depending on what other projects they've had to abandon to deal with your problem.

LET THE BUYER BEWARE—
MAKING SURE YOU GET WHAT YOU WANT FROM A CONTRACTOR OR CRAFTSMAN

The only real guarantee you have of good work is to be able to control as much of the process of doing it or getting it done as possible. And with contractors and craftsmen, the best leverage you have is money. That's why the payment schedules we've discussed and keeping track of the job while it's in progress are so important. If you can see that the cabinetry in the kitchen isn't going in the way you want it to, you need to address the issue before the installation is finished—and certainly before you make future payments to the contractor.

It's also essential that you do your homework on materials and products that are going to be used on the job, so you know exactly what you're getting. For instance, it's easy to know if you're going to like the prefabricated kitchen cabinetry suggested by the contractor—go to the kitchen outlet with him and look at what you've chosen in the flesh. If the contractor is building the cabinetry from scratch, make sure you've seen detailed plans and ask him to bulid or show you a sample, so you can see for sure it's going to be what you want.

INDEX